THE OFFICIAL
COMPANION
SEASON FOUR

SHARON GOSLING

TITAN BOOKS

BATTLESTAR GALACTICA:
THE OFFICIAL COMPANION SEASON FOUR

ISBN: 9781845769383

Published by
Titan Books
A division of
Titan Publishing Group Ltd
144 Southwark Street
London SE1 0UP

First edition October 2009
2 4 6 8 10 9 7 5 3 1

THANKS TO

First of all, David Bassom, for all your help, support and contacts. I hope I didn't let you down, David — you're a star. Thanks to all the interviewees for finding time to talk to me despite your busy schedules, especially Ron Moore, David Eick, Michael Rymer, Michael Taylor, Michael Nankin, Jane Espenson, Seamus Kevin Fahey, Gary Hutzel, Jesse Tovey and Wayne Rose. Thanks to Maril Davis at Ron Moore's office, James Halpern at David Eick's office, and Perla Aboulache at Edward James Olmos' office. Thanks to the lovely Cath Trechman for making sure I didn't write complete rubbish. Last but certainly not least, thank you to Admiral Edward James Olmos for writing a spiffing foreword. SO SAY WE ALL!

Below photo on page 155 courtesy of Mike Bieke.

DEDICATION
For my favourite Finn, Kati "Out of the box is where I live" Clements, whom I would back in a fight against Starbuck any day.

Visit our website:
www.titanbooks.com

What did you think of this book? We love to hear from our readers. Please email us at reader **feedback@titanemail.com** or write to us at the above address.
You can also visit us at **www.titanbooks.com**

To receive advance information, news, competitions, and exclusive Titan offers online, please register as a member by clicking the "sign up" button on our website: **www.titanbooks.com**

A CIP catalogue record for this title is available from the British Library.

Printed and bound in the USA.

[CONTENTS]

T hus starts the final documentation of one of the most intriguing and incredible journeys recorded on film… for the time has come to write the last foreword… or should I say… the final "log" in the Admiral's Journal:

June 19th of the year 2009:

Today, I stood amongst those who most deserve to read this memoir, our loyal fans! I received thanks upon thanks by the thousands today in Philadelphia, at a Convention that housed the dreams, soul and imagination of a people. People so committed to the world of Comic Books and Science Fiction that they travel the world to participate in ComiCons.

When asked to write this foreword as the *Admiral of the* Galactica, I was honored and humbled by the request.

Ron Moore, Mary McDonnell and Jamie Bamber wrote the previous forewords. They gave an incredible insight into what it took to create the past seasons of *Batttlestar Galactica*. They gave thanks to all who took part in this undertaking. From the Studios and the Executives to the entire Pre-Production, Production and Post-Production staff and support systems. And… especially… to all our families.

I, too, would like to thank everyone who had anything to do with the making of *Battlestar Galactica*.

This entry into the final journal is DEDICATED to the millions of LOYAL FANS,

from around the world, who supported us and helped to create a very unique (and first of its kind) experience in the creative life of a television program.

The process in the creation of Television and/or Film projects starts with the story idea and then germinates from there. The Writers expound on the idea until they have a treatment. This quickly turns into the structure. This is where the fun really begins, or should I say the magic. Imagination runs without limits, infusing the Writer with laughter and joy, panic and fear, with strength and courage!

Through the evolvement of the story, into the driving pace of the characters' voices, life flows into an idea and thus becomes the SCRIPT (a very unique reading experience). If you have never read one, do so!

Next, the script goes to the studio for their notes. After back-and-forth note giving, the script goes to the production team. The Director, along with the Actors, breaks down the script.

All through the process the Writers answer every possible question given to them by everyone involved with the production. Department heads try to envision the needs placed on their respective crafts. The script then enters a new stage. That of realisation! We start to film!

Here, the magic either happens or it doesn't. If it does, the script becomes the documentation of human behavior, and scenes embody emotion and elevate the written word. The Writers see the depth of their work come to life. A beautiful event that everyone around the set loves to experience, and which drives this art form. We call it "breathing life into the page." The Director guides all aspects of the filming, until we reach the final take on the final day of shooting. A cheer breaks out as the words "That's a wrap…" reverberate from the First Assistant Director.

All the elements created by the Production team move on to the Post Production unit. The metamorphosis of the story continues, but at a much more intense pace. The assemblage, during the editing process, gives a new understanding to the story. The construct of the pieces creates a much clearer vision. By the time Paul Leonard (Head of Post Production), Andy Seklir (Supervising Editor), Gary Hutzel (Visual Effects Supervisor) and Bear McCreary (Composer) are done, and everyone goes into the final mix with all the elements, the work has moved to a very intense and beautiful experience. The MAGIC is in full swing and everyone who sees it is energised.

The story has been realised to its fullest and augmented every step of the way. Each step making the story more vivid! More intense!! More real!!!

It is complete.

NOW…. The show is aired to the world on Television.

Here is where the incredible alchemy* took place, creating a totally unpredictable and profound impact on *Battlestar Galactica*'s FUTURE. No one could've predicted or imagined it.

Immediately, and I mean seconds not minutes after the airing, it is downloaded onto the Internet! Those that know how to do it, and there are millions, begin to watch the episode. All over the world people are watching it almost simultaneously.

The world begins to BLOG! And the meaning of every frame of BATTLESTAR GALACTICA is diagnosed, scrutinised and embellished with human emotion and love. Critiques that can only be found in the deepest regions of the FANbase travel the world and, you guessed it, it takes over. Like no one has ever known before. True alchemy.

But now another MIRACLE appears. The writers of the SHOW are leading the BLOGS. They converse and CHAT.

Interpreting… commenting… thanking… and LISTENING.

Yes, LISTENING to the world share its insight on what they had just experienced. Taking the themes even higher than all the pre-production, production and post-production could achieve. Taking it further. To a place that no art form of this kind had ever explored. Ron, David and the incredible Writing team, moved forward from THIS point, and continued to explore this world.

*Alchemize: *to transform something into gold OR into a much purer or brighter form by alchemy.*

Yes, we gave the show all our heart and soul. Yes, we gave it all our expertise. Everyone who touched it, gave it their ALL! But the FANS gave us life.

By Blogging… WHAT IT MEANT TO YOU… Not with ego! Not with malice! Nor with any ill intent!… But with the same love for the world that all the writers, the crafts people… EVERYONE… who touched and imagined this experience created.

And if the old saying that "Intent equals Content" rings true, then the Fans elevated the show because of your INTENT.

So you see…. This may be the final "LOG"… but it is not THE END! For we all know now that the world of *Battlestar Galactica* was created and nurtured by all, and that WE will visit it and reflect for years to come because our intentions were pure…. We gave of ourselves to this form and now it LIVES! FOREVER!

Thank you to all… especially the FANS…

For this truly is once-in-a-life-time…

They do have a… PLAN!

SO SAY WE ALL

Admiral William "Husker" Adama
Battlestar *Galactica*

(As read to Colonel Saul Tigh on the flight home from Philadelphia.)

[THERE MUST BE SOME WAY OUT OF HERE...]

"It's just been a tremendous joy in my life, this show. I really didn't anticipate or even hope that it was going to be as great an experience as it was. I think the show itself really does take the vision I had at the beginning and actually make it happen." — Ronald D. Moore

The idea of ending a project of such magnitude as *Battlestar Galactica* was daunting for the writers and producers on many levels. It had kept Ronald D. Moore, David Eick and their team of writers and producers busy for half a decade or more, not to mention the hundreds of other craftspeople involved in physically getting the series to the screen. It was still hugely popular all over the world, garnering attention from mainstream press as well as enjoying strong genre support. Other science fiction series had run well beyond the four-and-a-half years that *Battlestar Galactica* had been on the air, so was season four really the right place to end *Galactica*'s journey through space?

"I was pretty determined that was the end," says Ron Moore. "It was a dawning decision over the course of the third season. I started feeling like there's probably only one season left, and by the time I got to the end of the third season, I was convinced that it was time to bring the story to the end."

"If you're going to be truthful and honest about it, which was always our intention from the beginning," adds executive producer David Eick, "the nature of the idea had a finite limitation to it. You're setting out to find Earth — at a certain point you're going to find it, or you're not, and if you're not then it's a different show, because they're looking for something else for some other reason."

Below: Three of *Galactica*'s Cylon crew.

The feeling was that the story had run its natural course, and to push on into a fifth year, or perhaps even beyond, would extend the narrative beyond its natural length. Despite the writers' talents, pushing beyond that boundary could only diminish the impact of the central tale they had originally set out to tell.

"That acknowledgement was the first conversation," admits Eick. "'Okay, are we *sure* we want this to be the end? Why do we feel it's important to end it now? What are the drawbacks? Is there a story we are leaving on the table that we will wish later that we had explored?' That particular story had reached its third act. Every nook and

cranny felt like it had been explored, the mission had been stretched out and really investigated from a creative standpoint as thoroughly as we could, and, at a certain point, as much as *Battlestar Galactica* had always been a character-driven show, your longevity is still driven in part by your story. Even though the characters could have gone on and on and on, the *story* had reached its conclusion. That's why we knew we had to end the show. And that was the nerve centre of our discussion as we headed into the fourth season."

Once it had been definitively decided that the fourth year would be *Battlestar Galactica*'s last, the question became: how to conclude such an epic show in a satisfactory way. Moore already knew where he wanted *Galactica*, her crew and the surviving human fleet to end up. But how to get them there?

"The big thing was that we bring resolution to the series and try to tie up as many of the plot threads as we could, and as many as we thought we *should*," says Moore, recalling those early pre-production discussions. "We knew some basic things. We knew that we wanted *Galactica* to get to Earth in the distant past, we knew that Adama was going to make it, we knew that Laura would die, we knew that... actually, now I think about it, there wasn't too much beyond that," he laughs. "Those were the major things, and a lot of the rest of the fourth season came up in the discussions, [for example] finding the original Earth first, mid-season."

There were also practical story points that the writers' room needed to work out as a result of the conclusion to season three. Having revealed who four of the final five

Above: Kara's confusion caused her volatile tendencies to explode in season four.

Cylons were, certain character adjustments had to be made and explained. The most significant of these was Tyrol's son, Nicky.

"It was mostly just combing through the back-stories and trying to make them consistent and make sure that we had plausible explanations for contradictions that might crop up," Moore explains. "For a time we were even willing to have Tyrol and Cally's child be half-Cylon and half-human. At the outset we kind of said, 'Okay, well there's two of them — we'll have to figure out what that means later'. Then we just decided that we didn't want to do it. But there weren't a lot of major shifts that we had to do in the aftermath. When we chose them as the final Cylons, we had a long discussion about whether there was anything in their back-story or anything that had been established about them that would preclude it, and we realised that no, there wasn't. So it didn't take too much patching over as a result of that."

Before the production reached the momentous climax of the finale, however, they had to negotiate some tricky events off-screen that could have been prematurely fatal for the series. As *Battlestar Galactica*'s fourth season went before the cameras, rumblings began to reach the industry as a whole that a WGA (Writers Guild of America) strike was in the offing. The strikers aimed to redress the imbalance between the remuneration that writers received in comparison with what the large studio corporations earned from the writers' work. In the case of *Battlestar Galactica*, a strike would effectively mean that the production would have to close down entirely. Since all of the show's writers were also producers who had a hand in the editing of the series (in itself a form of writing), none of them would be able to work on the show at all during the strike.

In the event, the strike was finally called just as *Battlestar Galactica* was preparing to go on mid-season hiatus. In theory, this was a good thing — the production would have temporarily shut down for a month or so anyway at this point. Usually, however, the writers would have used this period to work on the scripts for the back half of the season, which in this case they could not do. There was also a very real fear that should the strike continue for three or four months, the studio would not be able to continue paying the costs for a production that wasn't working — even though the show wasn't filming, all of the staff on the payroll still needed to be paid, and the standing sets were in stages that had to be rented, whether they were being used or not.

Above: Politics once again took a central role in the show's storyline.

"We were terrified at certain points, when the strike looked like it was going to go on for a long time, that someone at the studio or the network would pull the plug on *Battlestar Galactica* altogether," recalls David Eick, who was by that time executive producing *Bionic Woman*, and dealing with similar worries on that show. "The last episode would have been the last one we shot, period."

"I flew up to Vancouver and gathered the cast and crew together and told them what had happened," recalls Ron Moore, who was a prominent advocate of the strike. "That we, the writers, were on strike, but I wanted them to complete the episode, and I wanted them to do the best job they could. I didn't expect them to walk in solidarity to the writers — they had their own families to take care of. But there weren't going to be any more scripts, and there weren't going to be any more script pages, so they were pretty much on their own. As a result, those episodes were full of a lot of intense emotions from the cast and crew, because they were worried that maybe these were the last *Galactica*s that they would ever get to shoot. It was a very tough time."

The episode on the lot as the strike began was 'Sometimes a Great Notion', slated as the first episode of the second half of the season, and a particularly bleak story following the revelation of Earth as a desolate, uninhabitable wasteland.

[THERE MUST BE SOME WAY OUT OF HERE...]

"It was poignant," recalls Jamie Bamber. "We (the cast) were all in the same place, which is rare. We had two whole days, and we treated it as the end. We had a big dinner afterwards and we said goodbye to each other. It *was* an ending. We had found Earth, and Earth was a wasteland. Actually, that's the ending that I think I would have written had I been writing the show. It felt right and wrong at the same time."

Moore doesn't agree that the mid-season two-parter would have formed an ideal ending. "I think it would have been very sad," he says. "It would have been unsatisfying. I mean, at the end [of the episode] they keep going, and I suppose that's a legitimate ending, but it would have been very tragic, I think, for everyone involved with the production."

In the event, the strike lasted three months and, although *Battlestar Galactica*'s fate was far from assured for much of that time, the studio found a way to keep the production alive. "The only good thing that came out of it was that it gave me a chance to re-think some elements of the second half of the season, things that I realised probably weren't going to work as well," says Moore. "When the strike was over I brought the writers in and said, 'Let's re-break some of the scripts that we've already decided to do — I don't think some of these story elements are going to work.' So we sort of revamped a big chunk of the storyline going into the second half."

Something else had happened during the prolonged hiatus that shook the production. Michael Trucco, who had become such an integral part of the series since his introduction as Samuel Anders, suffered a near-fatal car accident in which he broke his neck. "It was devastating. I spoke to him the next day. He was in traction and sounded like someone who had just been through a war. But his spirits were still very high," recalls Eick. "I will never forget him telling me that when he got out of the car, he could feel that there was something wrong with his neck, like it was kinked. He kept asking people who had gathered around the scene of the accident to pull on his arms, like he wanted to crack a knuckle or something. And no one would do it, because they were afraid of doing something horrible [to him]. He didn't realise it at the time, but learned later from his doctor that had anyone taken him up on that, he probably would never have walked again."

The fact that Trucco had managed to get himself out of the totalled car was a miracle in itself. Doctors later said that they had no idea how he had managed to move, as he'd suffered very similar injuries to those that had left *Superman* star

Below: The writers had intended to explore the story of Baltar's cult further, but time pressures did not allow for expansion.

Christopher Reeve paraplegic. The producers' immense relief that the young actor was alive and (in relative terms, at least) well was followed by practical worries about his return to work. Anders had, after all, become one of the series major characters. "It happened at a period of time when we were in a position to allow him to heal up for the most part," says Eick. "But he was still limited physically, and there were pain and flexibility issues — and, I would imagine, some emotional issues for anyone who has been through something like that."

Surprisingly, Moore reports that Anders' subsequent transformation into a hybrid wasn't as a result of Trucco's injury. "That didn't really happen until we were working on those last episodes," the writer explains. "But we were shooting episodes with him before that. We were plotting out episodes with him as one of the final five, and being involved in the mutiny and all that. It really wasn't until we were looking at episodes down the line, and from episode seventeen, where he would have a bullet in the brain and would start talking in terms of flashbacks and the missing back-story. He made an astonishing recovery and he had pretty much full mobility. He was moving around, running and doing things in the show before he took that bullet — and that was *after* the accident. So he was available as a completely mobile actor. It was only after that when we were working on subsequent stories that the idea of turning him into a hybrid came up. It wasn't done to immobilise him."

"I don't remember having a specific conversation about making Anders a hybrid just because we knew it would keep him immobile," agrees Eick. "Although this becomes a little bit chicken-and-egg in itself — were we talking about Anders and then we said, 'Hey this will work out even better than we thought'? Or were we not talking about Anders and then the accident happened and we thought, 'Well, he can remain in a reclining position, what can we give him?' But, for sure, it was a fortuitous role for him to be playing, because it required very limited mobility, although being in that soup and having to be in that make up and having to lie in the cold — there are more pleasant ways to spend your afternoon, regardless! But at least it allowed us to keep him in the show."

Having weathered two major storms, *Battlestar Galactica* headed for its finale with frightening pace and speed. Though Moore didn't want every question brought up during the show's run to be tied up with a neat little bow, there were certain story-lines that he had hoped to spend more time on. Some avenues, however, just had to be left unexplored.

"We wanted to get more into what was going on with Baltar and the cult down below decks," Moore explains. "We wanted more of an idea of what was happening in the fleet, on the other ships, and, as always, a lot of that got squeezed out. We also wanted to do more with Tyrol. We didn't get a lot of Tyrol stories going in the second half — there were various little things like that."

For the most part, though, Moore is happy with how the fourth season of *Battlestar Galactica* panned out. And in terms of giving an audience — and the industry as a whole — a glimpse of something different from the science fiction genre, the series certainly hit its mark.

"I don't know that I could have possibly imagined just how gratifying the experience would be and just how fulfilling it's been, and how well it's been received," says Moore, looking back at the extraordinary feat he and his production team achieved with *Battlestar Galactica*. "It's just been a tremendous joy in my life, this show. I really didn't anticipate or even hope that it was going to be as great an experience as it was. I think the show itself really does take the vision I had at the beginning and actually make it happen — I did see a show that was very much like this, that was dark, compelling, mature, that took science fiction seriously, that tackled really tough political and religious ideas and wasn't afraid of them, had a tremendous ensemble, and reinvented a lot of things in filmed science fiction. And, in that sense, it is what I wanted it to be from the outset. But in the way it has affected people, and the way it has affected my life and how great a journey it was — I really didn't even dare hope for how great it turned out to be." ∎

ALL ALONG THE WATCHTOWER

As it turns out, the key to Earth's survival (or at least, one of them) is legendary singer-songwriter Bob Dylan's haunting song 'All Along the Watchtower'. The musician himself is a somewhat fitting addition to the *Battlestar Galactica* pantheon. If the show can be read as a comment on the folly of the current human condition and our tendency for division along religious and cultural lines, then Dylan's music is a perfect soundtrack. In the sixties, when popular music was still a powerful tool for political comment, Dylan's songs — which reflected themes of social and political unrest — became anthems for both the civil rights movement and protests against the Vietnam War.

"It was a song I had been obsessed with for many years," laughs Moore, of why he chose Dylan's song. "I fell in love with it. I actually tried to do an entire *Roswell* episode about it when I worked on that show, and that never came to pass. But it just stuck with me, and I was always fascinated by the song. The lyrics are dense and fascinating, and it can be interpreted in a lot of different ways. When we started talking in terms of music being a key in the show, I just said, 'The song will be "All Along the Watchtower".' That was my first choice."

As revealed in this book's section about the episode 'Sometimes a Great Notion', there was originally a scene depicting Anders playing the song to his fellow Cylons back on Earth, 2000 years in the past. Had this scene been in the shooting script, it would have been one of the last filmed by Michael Trucco before his hiatus accident. It's a rather strange correlation with the song's origins, as 'All Along the Watchtower' was written by Dylan as he recovered from a motorcycle accident so significant to the musician's life that music historians use it as a demarcation in his career — Dylan's music is often divided into 'pre- and post-' accident work.

On a lighter note, for viewers wondering if the song's inclusion is a tribute to another genre classic, Moore confirms that it has absolutely nothing to do with *Watchmen*. ∎

Opposite: The divide between the Cylons was a key storyline for season four.

[RAZOR]

WRITTEN BY: Michael Taylor
DIRECTED BY: Félix Enriquez Alcalá

GUEST CAST: Michelle Forbes (Admiral Helena Cain), Graham Becket (Colonel Jack Fisk), Stephanie Jacobsen (Kendra Shaw), Nico Cortez (Young Adama), Matthew Bennett (Aaron Doral), Steve Bacic (Colonel Jurgen Belzen), Brad Dryborough (Hoshi), Eileen Pedde (Gunnery Sergeant Erin Mathias), Fulvio Cecere (Lieutenant Alastair Thorne, Vincent Gale (Peter Laird), Campbell Lane (The Hybrid), Kyra Scott (Young Helena Cain), Chandra Berg (Little Lucy Cain), Peter Flemming (Helena's father), Shaker Paleja (Medic Hudson), Andrew Dunbar (Marine DaSilva), Jacob Blair (Squad Leader Banzai), Peter Bryant (Frank Bruno)

"You're a step up. That doesn't change the fact that you're an outsider who was brought in to clean up our mess. Or the impression that your daddy just gave you a Battlestar like he was tossing you the keys to a new car." — Kendra Shaw

---

Having recently taken command of *Pegasus*, Lee Adama tries to gain the trust of her crew. One of Cain's officers is Kendra Shaw, a young and apparently promising young woman whom Lee chooses as his XO. He's intrigued by her personnel file, in which Cain praises her, but which seems to hint at disapproval from other quarters. Shaw herself remains tight-lipped, distant and cold, apparently loyal to Cain's memory. Flashbacks tell of Kendra's arrival aboard *Pegasus*, immediately prior to the Cylon attack, and her subsequent life under Cain's command. In the present day, Shaw clashes with Starbuck as *Galactica* investigates the disappearance of a missing science team who seem to have been captured by old-style Cylons. Admiral Adama recalls an incident he experienced in the first Cylon war, in which the Cylons experimented on captured humans, and determines to locate and rescue the missing crew. As Shaw's flashbacks continue, we learn that it was she who exposed the Six called Gina, who was involved in a romantic relationship with Cain. Shaw was also present when Cain ordered troops to board civilian vessels and strip them of their useful resources — whether or not the civilians were willing to cooperate.

In the present day, the rescue team, including Shaw and Starbuck, boards the Baseship where *Galactica* surmises the missing crew are being held, armed with a nuclear warhead that they will detonate remotely once the extraction has succeeded. When the warhead is damaged in a firefight, Lee orders Starbuck to stay behind to detonate it manually, knowing it means her certain death. Instead, an already-injured Shaw demands that Starbuck leave with the rescue team, detonating the nuke herself — and finally allowing herself to face what she did under Cain's command. In wanting to live up to her Commander's expectations, Shaw shot dead an unarmed civilian woman protesting at *Pegasus'* actions, instigating a massacre that she could not forget, nor forgive herself for.

Before season four got off the ground, the *Battlestar Galactica* production team provided viewers with a special two-hour movie event exploring the tumultuous events aboard *Pegasus* under the command of Admiral Cain. Designed to be an addition to, rather than a direct part of, the show's final year on air, 'Razor' aired on the SCI FI Channel and was also released as a DVD prior to season four beginning its run.

"It was more or less a cross-promotional opportunity for the show, in that it incorporated the home video division of NBC/Universal that was going to invest resources and marketing funds and visibility into *Battletar Galactica*," explains David Eick. "In so doing, we felt it was an opportunity to expose the show to a bigger audience. From a creative standpoint, we could tell a story from a different perspective — almost in a *Rashomon*-like fashion — going into a story that the audience had seen and known (or thought they had known) and showing a deeper understanding of it, a deeper point of view."

Above: 'Razor' filled in the background to the story of Cylon infiltrator Gina Inviere, explaining how she ended up battered and bruised in *Pegasus*' brig.

Above: Michelle Forbes' willingness to return to the show was a vital element in the writers' decision to return to *Pegasus*.

When the opportunity first arose, however, the notion of exploring further the situation aboard *Pegasus* under Admiral Cain was not the first idea that sprang to mind. The writer who would be charged with penning the movie was Michael Taylor. Taylor, a veteran science fiction scribe from series such as *Star Trek: Deep Space Nine*, *Star Trek: Voyager* and *Dead Zone*, had joined the writing staff of *Battlestar Galactica* during season three.

"We were telling our main story in our series, so we weren't going to in any way cramp that or cut into that storyline," Taylor recalls. "So we had to do something that we hadn't seen, that had happened in the past. We all started talking about it, and I was very drawn, at the beginning, to doing something that could hark all the way back to the first Cylon war and a young Bill Adama. But we all continued talking. The idea of an alternate timeline [came up]: a story where our characters somehow forestall the apocalyptic attack of the Cylons. That started being discussed, but that was too *Star Trek*. Our show does not deal with time travel or alternate reality. It *is* reality — we try to keep it as real as we can."

"I do remember there were other possibilities," agrees Moore. "We started talking about doing a character piece — Doc Cottle's log, or something, and they would be from his gruff perspective about different things that were happening in the fleet. We [also] talked about doing something where everything took place before the Miniseries began."

Once those ideas had been examined and discarded, it didn't take long for talk to move towards the *Pegasus*. The ship had been destroyed in the series proper, meaning that the only way to include it would be in a story that took place outside the timeline of the main series. Since the writers were looking for just such a story to tell, the opportunity there was obvious. Couple that with the fact that Admiral Cain had been one of the most intriguing guest characters created for the series, and that the cast and crew enjoyed working with actress Michelle Forbes, and the writers' room had found their subject. "The *Pegasus* and Cain came to the fore and there wasn't much discussion on any other front," says Moore. "That quickly took us to Admiral Cain, and talking about going back before the attack."

"That was the story to tell," Taylor adds, simply. "The story of another starship, which, under the same circumstances but under a different commander, went in a very different direction. And had a very different attitude and approach to dealing with the war, one that was even more aggressive and morally questionable and yet at the same time debateable."

Having secured Forbes' assurances that she was interested in returning to *Galactica* ("She loved the role she played, she loved *Battlestar Galactica*, and she was super happy to be able to come back," says Taylor), work went ahead on the script. Taylor decided that rather than tell the story entirely from Cain's point of view, 'Razor' would work better told through the eyes of someone under her command. This choice allowed Taylor to create the character of Kendra Shaw, a raw yet tough recruit who finds herself under the uncompromising command of Cain.

"It's wonderful to create a character from scratch," Taylor laughs. "I came into the show in the third season, so all the main players were already in place, and I just learned who they were and how to write their voices and got to know them as characters. But here was a chance to create a brand new character, so it was a wonderful opportunity for me. I knew I wanted it to be another strong female character, but I did not want her to be like Starbuck. I wanted her to be different and, if anything, to clash with Starbuck and in some ways be even tougher than Starbuck. But how did she get that way? How did this young woman get to be that hard, that quickly?"

For Taylor, the crux of Kendra Shaw's story was brought into focus once he had decided on the movie's title. 'Razor' is a reference to the first episode featuring Admiral Cain, 'Pegasus', in which Cain, intending to assassinate Adama, calls for a team of perfectly effective troops from her own command to execute her wishes — she wants 'razors'. The word, applied to a human operative, conjures up the idea of a sharp, incisive, almost clinical ability to get the job done. The question of how a soldier could become a razor was the catalyst Taylor's story needed to begin.

"The idea of a young woman that Cain would take under her wing, in a way, and mould into a razor — what did it take to *make* a razor, someone who could do what was deemed necessary without a moment's hesitation? With no moral quibbles, or complications? With no guilt?" the writer asks. "Well, that proved to be impossible, ultimately.

So that was a story about making a razor, and that plugged me into the character as well. Understanding who she was, and what she might have gone through to get to where she was."

The episode also featured a series of scenes that formed part of a series of 'webisodes' and explored Bill Adama's experiences as a young man in the first Cylon war. Adama as a youth was not something that *Battlestar Galactica* had brought to the screen before.

"I thought of him as the young, untested warrior — the guy itching to get into battle," says Taylor, of how he approached the character of Adama in order to write those scenes. "There's a movie called *The Great Waldo Pepper* with Robert Redford, in which he plays a pilot who was one of the most talented of his generation, but only got into WWI just as it ended; he never got to be an ace. I don't know if I was thinking of that movie, but I tried to think of Adama as someone who had been itching to get into this war, and finally he gets in there on the last day — and it's a much different experience to what he imagined."

Of course, having decided that 'Razor' would feature a very young Adama, the production needed to find an actor capable of taking on the role. It was, says David Eick, no easy task. "Not only was it a physical match that we were looking for, we were also looking for someone with the gravitas of the Adama character, that Edward James Olmos brings to him, and that doesn't grow on trees! So it was definitely a difficult search."

Eventually, the production found young actor Nico Cortez, who had previously appeared in guest-starring roles on shows such as *Alias* and *CSI*. "I thought he was amazing," says Wayne Rose, who was charged with directing the additional webisode scenes. "He really took it very seriously. He spent as much time [researching] as he could beforehand. He watched as much as he could of Eddie, and he tried to do the little things that Adama did. He's a fairly green actor, which in a way was good. We could really push him where we wanted to push him, although," Rose laughs, "sometimes, when he was doing his William 'Husker' Adama voice, you had to pull him back a little bit! But he worked really hard at it. He was willing to do anything I asked him to do."

Michael Taylor reveals that although the movie was shot exactly as scripted — and that the shooting script did not differ dramatically from his earlier drafts — in editing, 'Razor' underwent significant changes. Most notably, the movie's structure altered completely. "The script was very linear, very chronological," explains the writer. "It starts near the end, then flashes back to the very beginning, to young Adama's war, and continues building in that way. In editing, we realised that we were missing our regular characters, we were too long without them — in the script we didn't get them until the last third of the show."

'Razor' had in part been designed to work for an audience that was not intimately aware of the *Battlestar Galactica* series. But the writer and producers felt that without a more immediate look at how the events of Shaw's life with Cain impacted on the main characters lives in the present, the movie lacked a way to base it within the

show's reality. In the editing room, as they puzzled over how best to fix this problem, inspiration came from another *Battlestar Galactica* veteran.

"Michael Rymer, who didn't even direct this movie, was working on another episode," recalls Taylor. "He poked his head in the doorway of the editing suite and said, 'Well, what if you made the last third of the show the frame for the whole show?' That brought it all into focus in post production. We were like, 'Yes, let's start amidst our characters and then flash back all over the place to flesh out our story, to show how we got to this point.' And that very much grounded the show."

In deciding to re-cut the edit to intersperse the *Galactica* scenes throughout the story, other elements of the movie had to be dropped. One of these was a voice-over that Taylor had included, in which Kendra Shaw described her thoughts and feelings as her life aboard *Pegasus* went on. Also trimmed was a spectacular action sequence that Taylor had devised as an opening for the movie.

"The thing that I missed most was the original opening of the show, which was very different," says Taylor. "It was a flash-forward to the near the end of the show, and the final bloody show-down with the old-style Cylons on their Baseship. It was a very *Apocalypse Now* shoot 'em up. When we were looking for our actress to play Kendra Shaw, David Eick said, 'We need a movie-star opening, something bigger.' So I found something and wrote it, and really fell in love with it. But it did not fit into the new structure. So there are glimpses of it in the course of the show towards the end, but it's no longer at the beginning. That's the biggest thing I missed. I happen to have the only DVD copy, I think, of a cut that still has that beginning!" ■

Above: Writer Michael Taylor enjoyed creating the character of Kendra Shaw (Stephanie Jacobsen), and immediately decided to set her at odds with Kara Thrace.

[SEASON FOUR]

The Cylons were created by Man.

They rebelled.

They evolved.

They look and feel Human.

Some are programmed to think they are Human.

There are many copies...

And they have a plan.

THE CAST

Admiral William 'Husker' Adama: Edward James Olmos
President Laura Roslin: Mary McDonnell
Commander Lee 'Apollo' Adama: Jamie Bamber
Captain Kara 'Starbuck' Thrace: Katee Sackhoff
Dr Gaius Baltar: James Callis
Number Six: Tricia Helfer
Lt Sharon 'Athena' Agathon/Number Eight: Grace Park
Colonel Saul Tigh: Michael Hogan
Chief Galen Tyrol: Aaron Douglas
Captain Karl 'Helo' Agathon: Tahmoh Penikett
Lt Anastasia Dualla: Kandyse McClure
Lt Felix Gaeta: Alessandro Juliani
Cally Henderson-Tyrol: Nicki Clyne
Ensign Samuel T. Anders: Michael Trucco
Tory Foster: Rekha Sharma

THE CREW

Developed by: Ronald D. Moore
Executive Producers: Ronald D. Moore and David Eick
Co-Executive Producers: Michael Angeli, Jane Espenson, Michael Taylor and Mark Verheiden
Supervising Producers: Bradley Thompson and David Weddle
Producers: Harvey Frand, Ron E. French and Michael Rymer
Co-producer: Paul M. Leonard
Associate Producers: James Halpen, Sian McArthur and Andrew Seklir
Consulting Producer: Glen A. Larson
Based on the series _Battlestar Galactica_ created by: Glen A. Larson
Production Designer: Richard Hudolin
Art Director: Douglas McLean
Visual Effects Supervisor: Gary Hutzel
Director of Photography: Stephen McNutt
Costume Designer: Glenne Campbell
Music: Bear McCreary

[HE THAT BELIEVETH IN ME]

WRITTEN BY: Bradley Thompson and David Weddle
DIRECTED BY: Michael Rymer

GUEST CAST: Ryan Robbins (Charlie Connor), Keegan Connor Tracy (Jeanne), Leah Cairns (Lieutenant Margaret 'Racetrack' Edmondson), Heather Doerksen (Marine #2), Lara Gilchrist (Paulla Schaffer), Colin Corrigan (Marine Allan Nowart), Lukas Pummell (Derrick), Leela Savasta (Tracey Anne), Shaun Omaid (Shaunt)

"You've got to trust me on this one." — Kara Thrace

Stunned by the reappearance of the presumed-dead Kara Thrace, Lee Adama returns to his defence of the fleet. As the *Galactica* begins to suffer heavy losses, Anders has a strange moment of communion with a Cylon Raider. After looking him in the eye, it peels away and the Cylons abruptly withdraw. Back on *Galactica*, Kara, who thinks she's only been gone a few hours, says she knows the way to Earth. Roslin urges Adama to think of her return as a Cylon trap. Starbuck can't give Adama Earth's coordinates, but says she has a 'feeling' of how to get there. Adama refuses to follow her recommendations, and begins to jump away from the nebula. With each jump Kara experiences head pain, and says she's losing the way back.

Elsewhere on *Galactica*, Baltar discovers that a group of women have formed a cult around him. One asks him to pray for her deathly sick child. Later, Baltar's sincerity is challenged by Six — he is attacked by a group of men, and she demands to know whether his prayers for the child were genuine. He says they were, and later discovers that the child has been miraculously cured. Meanwhile, a distraught Kara continues to beg Adama to turn *Galactica* around. When he continues to refuse, she decides it's down to Roslin's influence, and the President must be removed...

Having made the decision in pre-production that season four would definitively be *Battlestar Galactica*'s final year on air, the writing team were confronted with an added sense of gravitas in considering how the season would pan out. There would be no more after this: this was the end. And so season four, at a very basic level, had to be different in style to previous seasons. "This season was very different because it was the last season, and we knew going into it that we were going to structure it as one long story. I said that from the beginning," Ron Moore revealed in his podcast that accompanied the show's broadcast. "I gave up any pretence that this season was going to be about anything other than one long story of all these characters — where they had been and getting to Earth."

Opposite: Lee's joy at Kara's return outweighed any questions of just where she had been for three months.

SURVEILLANCE: ADDITIONAL

A scene that was cut from the script before it was shot showed Kara returning to the locker room for the first time to discover Anders' name replacing hers on her locker door. Starbuck then discovered that all her stuff had been given away in her absence — which to her is just a few hours — and she's not best pleased. Though a fun sequence, ultimately it was decided that due to time constraints and plot flow, it wasn't needed.

In a season full of shocks, the first was the reappearance of Starbuck, apparently alive and well. Fans had been devastated by the apparent destruction of Kara Thrace at the end of season three, and yet here she was, alive and well. Or was she? Debate about what Starbuck was raged on throughout the season for both the audience and the *Galactica* crew — one script read-through was famously interrupted by Katee Sackhoff's frustration in not knowing how to play this character that suddenly seemed to be entirely alien to her. The producers' response was: "That's how you play it. Starbuck's as confused as you are."

In fact, the writers knew exactly what Starbuck was — Moore literally wanted her to have died and returned from the dead. But more explanation than that, he felt, would have muddied the waters. An early idea that perhaps only Lee could see her (*à la* the Six in Baltar's head) was toyed with but eventually discarded. Far better to play off the confusion engendered by her literal return.

And what confusion Starbuck's return caused, particularly amongst those characters closest to her. Some accepted her without question (Lee Adama) some desperately wanted to accept her (Admiral Adama) and some flatly refused to accept her as anything other than a Cylon trick (Laura Roslin). These attitudes towards her allowed the writers to play with some significant role reversals. The two Adamas, both traditionally practical, didn't want to deal with another loss and desperately wanted to believe their loved one had indeed returned. While Roslin, whose spirituality was responsible for *Galactica*'s mythic quest for Earth, became the sceptic.

"I think, as I experienced her, it was 'There has to be someone keeping an eye on this,'" says Mary McDonnell, of Roslin's refusal to accept the proof of her eyes. "And quite often, that someone has to be the President. If this was a trick, it would be a disaster, and there wasn't really any information that Laura had to convince her otherwise. So I think, particularly because she felt everyone else was *so* willing to see it as a spiritual event, she took the more practical way. It was worth it for her to risk [it] in case this was not Kara Thrace. It was a more practical, cautious, and somewhat cynical point of view."

Already known to the audience, of course, is the fact that Roslin's suspicions are moving in the wrong direction. The four Cylons revealed at the conclusion of season three are shown to be struggling with the revelation of their true nature, much as the actors were themselves. "Two of them went through absolute denial and hated the idea and then came round and realised it was the best thing that could ever happen to their characters," recalls Jamie Bamber, "and two of them were ancillary characters anyway, and realised they were going to be major players, and were delighted. I think I would have gone through a similar process to Michael [Hogan] and Aaron [Douglas]. I would have said: 'You can't do this to my character, it's not right, it's not fair.' But that's an indication of how attached they were to their characters, and that's right, because you've been playing this thing for so long, and you realise that everything you've been playing is off the mark. It's a bit like having a big rug pulled out from under your feet."

"I liked the disparate reaction of the four," says Michael Trucco. "Tory embraced it. She'd been this wallflower as a human being and suddenly she had this new sense of identity and power, which I thought was great for her. Tyrol had this sense of resignation: that was the cruel hand of fate just catching him as the butt of a joke — 'There you go, wasn't that typical? Now I'm a Cylon. Okay.' And with Tigh it was the anger and the refusal, the denial. With Anders it was confusion and fierce loyalty to Starbuck regardless of whether he was human or Cylon. He was still, I think, driven by love."

The scene in which Anders shares a strange moment with the Cylon Raider changed dramatically in post production. Originally, the scene had called for a much larger moment. But once the scene was shot, the producers realised it wasn't working in the way they had envisioned, and so visual effects supervisor Gary Hutzel and his team reworked the sequence. "Originally, as shot, the idea was yes, there's a face-off, but as we first designed it, it was in the middle of a larger action scene, and that's really as it was written," Hutzel explains. "It remained in a large action scene, but we had originally designed the sequence to have the Raiders come in as a flock and surround him. So he's chasing a Raider, he loses his cool — but then there's a pause in the action, and when we came back we found him basically surrounded by these Raiders that have gathered around him. He doesn't know quite what to make of that, and then they just break off and leave. We developed a whole sequence for that, but as we got into it, it was decided that there wasn't enough communion between his character and the Raiders. So that's when we developed the whole 'eye' thing. We went in and processed the regular live action footage to slow it down by about a factor of five or six. We created the slow motion entirely in post, because it was shot as a regular twenty-four-frame live action scene." ■

SURVEILLANCE: ADDITIONAL

Gaius Baltar's path in season four took him to a dramatically different place, and in this episode we get the first inklings of that transformation. From a non-believer, he becomes a preacher of monotheism and the leader of a cult of mainly female followers. When the writing team began to talk about the idea of Baltar finding himself surrounded by believers, they realised this cult would need a regular place to meet, and since Baltar's release from the brig, a place for him to live, as well. It made sense that the two converge, and in early discussions this central place was nicknamed 'Baltar's Lair'. The label stuck, and 'Baltar's Lair' was how the set was described in the scripts for season four.

[SIX OF ONE]

WRITTEN BY: Michael Angeli
DIRECTED BY: Anthony Hemmingway

GUEST CAST: Callum Keith Rennie (Leoben Conoy), Rick Worthy (Simon), Matthew Bennett (Aaron Doral), Sebastian Spence (Lieutenant Noel 'Narcho' Allison), Dean Stockwell (John Cavil), Bodie Olmos (Lieutenant Brenden 'Hotdog' Costanza), Tiffany Lyndall-Knight (The Hybrid), Leah Cains (Lieutenant Margaret 'Racetrack' Edmonson), Eileen Peddle (Gunnery Sergeant Erin Mathias), Jennifer Halley (Ensign Diana 'Hardball' Seelix), Colin Corrigan (Marine Allan Nowart)

"Stay in the room. Get out of my head." — William Adama

Kara Thrace holds President Roslin at gunpoint before handing her the gun and telling her to shoot her dead if Roslin really believes Kara to be a Cylon. Roslin shoots, but misses at point-blank range, just as the security guards enter and take Kara prisoner. In the brig, Kara's insistence that they are going the wrong way sends her into mania. Adama visits her, his anger spilling over as he tells her no one will help her now.

Meanwhile, the Cylons are facing their own problems. Cavil wants to lobotomise the Raiders to stop them refusing to attack the fleet now that they know the final five are among the humans. A vote splits the Cylon concensus — Numbers One, Four and Five vote for, while the Twos, Sixes and Eights vote against. Boomer sides with Cavil against her number. A Six named Natalie removes the inhibitors from the Centurions, telling them what Cavil is doing. The Centurions side with the Sixes, Twos and Eights, killing Cavil and his supporters. On *Galactica*, Lee leaves the ship to take his place on the Quorum as the four Cylons try to work out who the final Cylon could be. Believing that Baltar knows, they send Tory to seduce him.

Despite Roslin's protests, Adama gives Kara the *Demetrius* and a crew that includes Helo, Athena, Anders and Felix Gaeta. He instructs her to try to find Earth.

As if to prove that he meant what he said about season four being one large story, the action of 'Six of One' picks up right where the opening episode left off, with Kara holding Laura at gunpoint.

"I interpret the fact that she missed in that she just didn't want to shoot her, ultimately," laughs McDonnell, of Laura managing to miss Kara despite shooting her at close range. "There was an inability in her consciousness. I think the part of her that was trying to protect civilisation wanted to shoot her. She wanted to stop this. But another part of Laura could not get it right. The gun went so deeply against her grain that I just don't think she was successful."

Opposite: Adama tries to understand the welcome return of his "daughter".

Above: Starbuck and the Admiral discuss her "death" and three-month absence from *Galactica*.

In fact, the action in which Roslin shoots at Starbuck was debated extensively before the final draft of the script went into production. A very early draft did not have this beat in at all, and another featured Laura picking up the gun and trying to fire, but forgetting to take the safety off. Mary McDonnell had issues with this draft specifically, feeling that it made the President look stupid. Ultimately, Moore agreed with her, and the final version, in which Roslin's intentions are ambiguous, was created. Did she miss deliberately? Was it another act of fate? Is she just a really terrible shot?

"She was standing right in front of her, she shouldn't have missed her," McDonnell agrees. "We didn't really explore [her intentions] definitively in the writing. None of us were very sure — Ron just knew she missed, and that he didn't want her, ultimately, to shoot Kara. But I don't think any of us consciously committed to 'She missed on purpose.' From her point of view, I don't think she *chose* to miss, but perhaps unconsciously she did."

As the action of 'Six of One' bounces between *Galactica* and the events in the Cylon fleet, we see the opening event of the Cylon civil war, the repercussions of which echo throughout the season. One of the most interesting aspects of this is the insight the audience is given into the Cylon hierarchy. "One of the notions that sometimes gets lost in the show is that the Raiders themselves are as alive as the other Cylons," says Moore.

SURVEILLANCE: ADDITIONAL

The first draft of this script had Kara put in the brig with Caprica Six, as a symbol of her grouping with the other Cylons. The scene was intended to culminate in a slug-fest show-down between the two women, in a reprise of the fight between Starbuck and a Six model on Caprica in season one. It was eventually changed, as Ron Moore felt that it was being done simply to set up a fight between the two women, and the action would have been repeated when Adama took her out of one cell and put her into another for their own confrontation. In the end, it was rewritten.

"They simply exist in another level of sentience to the other Cylons."

Cavil's treatment of the Raiders was specifically designed to remind the audience that 'skinjobs' are only the most visible incarnation of the Cylon race — and illustrated how hard the writers had to work to keep all of the elements they had created in the *Battlestar Galactica* universe in focus for the audience. It's easy to forget that the Raiders and even the Centurions are so closely connected to the humanoid Cylons. Similarly, the human fleet is generally seen through the military prism of life on *Galactica*. Keeping the rest of the fleet in the mind of the audience would be a continual challenge for the writers throughout the series, and prompt some of the most significant events during the second half of the season.

One of the most unexpected moments in the episode occurs when Baltar suddenly finds himself confronted with 'Head Baltar'. It was the first time that James Callis had filmed a split-screen scene on *Battlestar Galactica*, but visual effects supervisor Gary Hutzel reports that the actor did an amazing job. So amazing, in fact, that most of the material shot was later edited for being too funny.

Above: Lee contemplates the turn his life is taking.

"What made the air was only a third of what was shot," Hutzel reveals. "He had a running dialogue with himself that was just hysterical. The dialogue was just so funny, his subtext for the two different characters was great, and his comedic timing was just brilliant. So we had fun cutting it all together and it was a great laugh in editorial. But when Ron saw it, it was like, 'Well, now I'm distracted, and I don't know what's going on in the scene any more because I'm now laughing my head off at Baltar.' So he pulled back. But the whole scene is just brilliant."

For Moore, one of the best interactions of the episode is the scene between Adama and Roslin in his quarters. It's a highly emotional and yet greatly restrained conversation, and one of the executive producer's high points in the entire season.

"These are scenes you have to wait a while in a series to get to," Moore told viewers in his podcast. "I don't think we could have taken these two characters to this place before now. We had to lay a lot of groundwork, we had to have travelled the long road with these people in order to justify getting to this place and for the actors to know their characters so well, to get them to take them to those places." ∎

SURVEILLANCE: ADDITIONAL

An earlier draft of the script featured Chief Tyrol inspecting Kara's Viper and discovering some strange hieroglyphs imprinted on its metal work. It was an intriguing idea, but the writers realised that they had no idea what it meant, and it would have required explaining at some point. To prevent writing themselves into a corner, the concept was dropped from the shooting script.

[THE TIES THAT BIND]

WRITTEN BY: Michael Taylor
DIRECTED BY: Michael Nankin

GUEST CAST: Richard Hatch (Tom Zarek), Donnelley Rhodes (Dr. Cottle), Matthew Bennett (Aaron Doral), Dean Stockwell (John Cavil), Jennifer Halley (Ensign Diana 'Hardball' Seelix), Christina Schild (Playa Palacious), Biski Gugushe (Sekou Hamilton), Finn R. Devitt (Nicky Tyrol), Donna Soares (Speaking Delegate #1), Andrew McIlroy (Jacob Cantrell), Judith Maxie (Picon Delegate), Iris Paluly (Speaking Delegate #2) Ryan McDonell (Lieutenant Eammon 'Gonzo' Pike), Marilyn Norry (Reza Chronicles)

> **"Well, sometimes a benevolent tyrant is exactly what you need."**
> **— Lee Adama**

Cavil resurrects and agrees to a conference with Natalie. She wants to unbox Three, who knows the identity of the final five. Cavil agrees, but then attacks. Elsewhere, Kara and the crew of the *Demetrius* have had no success finding Earth. Kara is still strung out, and the crew are becoming restless. On Colonial One, Lee takes his place as the Caprican delegate to the Quorum. Tom Zarek urges him to examine Roslin's political manoeuvres. He believes she is power-grabbing, and that democracy is being eroded by her close alliance with Adama and the military. Lee, listening, tries to raise a specific issue about the use of executive powers, but Roslin deflects the question.

On *Galactica*, a troubled and sleepless Cally Tyrol spies on her husband as he meets with Tory Foster. Later, she finds a note to Galen telling them where to meet. Thinking she'll catch him cheating on her, she spies on the meeting place, but instead discovers a worse truth — that Tigh, Tyrol, Foster and Anders are Cylons. Back home and beside herself, she beats Tyrol unconscious, then takes baby Nicky with the intention of committing murder-suicide. Tory talks her into handing over the baby before calmly blowing Cally out into the cold depths of space...

Opposite: Tom Zarek (Richard Hatch) tries to open Lee Adama's eyes to Roslin's "folly".

SURVEILLANCE: ADDITIONAL

The scene in which Admiral Adama sits silently with Tyrol after delivering the news about Cally's death originally had dialogue. However, on the day, the actors asked to film one take in silence. In editing, Ron Moore decided that this was in fact more poignant than the scripted scene, and so used it in the final cut.

'The Ties That Bind' is an expansive story, ranging from the epic beats leading up to the Cylon civil war to the small, intimate tragedies of one woman. Helmed by veteran *Battlestar* director Michael Nankin, the episode ultimately ties both sides of the story into the larger series arc, and also kicks off the all-important Cylon civil war.

"The negotiations between Cavil and the Sixes and the Sharons — that part of the story changed enormously, much to my ultimate disappointment," the director admits. "The thrust of that story originally, and during shooting, was the Centurions who had had their behaviour inhibitors removed. So all of the negotiation scenes

were designed to have CGI Centurions watching. The main focus wasn't the skin-jobs, it was the robots, because the story I was telling was not the negotiations, but the education of the Centurions, who were watching this political discussion and learning to lie. They were learning human traits from the skinjobs and there are all kinds of little cutaways, such as where Cavil, making a point, taps the table, and then behind him the Centurion is doing the same gesture."

This idea of the Centurions evolving was a storyline the writers had discussed as unfolding throughout season four. Ultimately, however, it was dropped, and as a result the focus of those scenes changed in editing. "We started putting it together, and the dialogue between the live action characters became wallpaper: you couldn't pay any attention to it," says visual effects supervisor Gary Hutzel. "You were so distracted by what the Centurions were doing that you had no idea what they were talking about. Ron came in and saw it and said, 'Well, we're not doing that.' So we ended up with a couple of Centurions in the background. We did keep Michael's notion of them listening in, though."

Because of the way the episode was shot, the removal of the Centurions impacted on the finished episode. "All the framing is off," explains Nankin. "There are all kinds of big holes in the frames, which were there for the Centurions."

The most shocking aspect of the episode, though, is the attempted suicide and then murder of distraught Specialist Cally. "That script cemented a trend that had been happening, in which I was the director responsible for killing most of the female cast," Nankin laughs. He had previously been responsible for filming Kara Thrace's demise in 'Maelstrom', for example, and would later direct Dualla's suicide. "It became a joke. Every time I turned up, actresses would run for cover. So when I read that Cally died, I thought, 'Oh my god. I'll never hear the end of it now!'"

Despite the downbeat nature of the script, Nankin realised there was a lot of room for visual experimentation. He was attracted to the idea of playing out Cally's gradual degeneration, and worked to find ways to represent her mental state on camera. "It told the story of a woman whose world was spinning out of control, a woman who was isolated from the rest of the world on *Galactica*," he says. "When she learns this secret, she's completely alienated, so I welcomed the challenge to find a way to visually tell that part of the story. The first was this idea of spinning out of control. I asked the props people to come up with one of

Opposite: Tyrol's already fragile emotional state is delt a devastating blow when he learns of Cally's death.

SURVEILLANCE: ADDITIONAL

In his podcast about this episode, Ron Moore reveals that 'The Ties That Bind' altered significantly during post-production. "I think ultimately the mistake that I probably made in structuring the story was that I leaned a little bit too much on the Cally story," he tells listeners. "I probably should have structured it as a sub-plot rather than the A-plot because I don't think it quite sustains itself."

As a result of the concerns Moore had, the episode underwent significant changes in post production. Originally, Tyrol's point of view was featured far more; to illustrate the struggle he was having adjusting to his Cylon nature, a huge part of his personality that he was unable to reveal to his already troubled wife. Some of the scenes depicting this still exist — for example, Tyrol staring at the sleeping Cally. Originally, this was part of a larger sequence that depicted the Chief hallucinating that he had murdered his wife and child as a result of his Cylon tendencies. In editing the episode and following his decision that Cally's suicide should be a B-plot rather than an A-plot, all of this was cut to pull events on the *Demetrius* and Lee Adama's first experiences as a politician to the fore.

those rotating children's room lights, and I got together with the DP, Steve McNutt, and started to work out a way to throw the illumination of this rotating light onto the walls, so that there was something visual that was actually spinning around her. Every time she's with her child, the room is literally spinning. The team that usually does the playback on all the monitors in the CIC created these stars and moons, so we had two projectors synced together so we could wash this over the entire set, and we could control the speed from shot to shot. So the episode starts with the image of these little star lights zooming around the room. And that tied into this motif of stars — I wanted to link the idea of stars to Cally, because at the end she ends up drifting in the stars. I wanted to foreshadow her fate in some way. So if you look, there are images of stars sprinkled through it, every time you see Cally."

Cally's attempted suicide and subsequent murder by Tory are exceptionally powerful scenes, and called on Gary Hutzel's team in their execution. Hutzel reveals that the footage that was shot ran far longer than ended up being used in the final edit. "There was a dialogue about how much of a meal we should make of her going down the launch tube," Hutzel recalls. "For me, there was a whole logic issue. She's being flushed out an airlock, she's got to go a *long* way — does she even *get* outside? We actually developed it so that you saw her body flying down the tube, her head smacking against the wall. Ultimately, when we showed that [to the producers], they felt it was the wrong beat for her."

Nicki Clyne's final appearance as Specialist Cally involved various aspects of visual effects that she hadn't been called on to try for *Battlestar Galactica* before. "We tried a bunch of different stuff, so there was a lot of preparation," says Hutzel. We shot her on wires and we shot her with wind in her hair at high speed to get her hair floating for the death shot outside."

Opposite: Lee takes his place on the Quorum and tries to mediate between Roslin and Zarek.

SURVEILLANCE: ADDITIONAL

The scene in which Cally mounts a dangerous expedition into the bones of *Galactica* was changed at the director's behest. "What was scripted was that she opens a panel and then rigs a speaker device so that she can overhear them electronically," Nankin explains. "I spent most of prep pushing another idea, which is the one where she squeezes through the bulkheads in the wall and is able to observe them. It was a part of the ship we had never seen, and it would add some danger because the crawl space wouldn't have a floor — there would just be a 100-foot drop. So it took four or five pleas to the writer and Ron Moore to try to get this going. When we built that part of the set, we actually brought Nicki Clyne down and didn't nail the walls in until we got her in there. We wanted to get exactly the size, so that it was truly difficult for her to get through. So we squished her in there, and then when she could barely move we said, 'Okay, that's where the wall goes!'"

The poignant image of Cally's dead body hanging in the void of space also changed from what had originally been discussed. "That shot was much more extended than it became in the show. We had tons and tons of footage of her floating, very little of which was used," reveals Hutzel, he adds that, originally, the idea had been to intercut more of that shot with the scene of Adama telling Tyrol about his wife's death. "I think Ron had a difficult time balancing that, figuring out how not to overdo that aspect of her death. And it did slow down the show; so I understand why he said, 'Let's move through this.' You see fourteen frames of her sucked out the airlock and then she's dead." ■

[ESCAPE VELOCITY]

WRITTEN BY: Jane Espenson
DIRECTED BY: Edward James Olmos

GUEST CAST: Keegan Connor Tracy (Jeanne), Leah Cains (Lieutenant Margaret 'Racetrack' Edmonson), Colin Lawrence (Lieutenant Hamish 'Skulls' McCall), Don Thompson (Specialist 3rd Class Anthony Figurski), Leela Savasta (Tracey Anne), Laura Gilchrist (Paulla Schaffer), Donna Soares (Speaking Delegate #1), Andrew McIlroy (Jacob Cantrell), Judith Maxie (Picon Delegate), Iris Paluly (Speaking Delegate #2), Marilyn Norry (Reza Chronicles), Lee Jeffery (Lieutenant Paolo 'Redwing' McKay)

"Sometimes the right thing is a luxury." — Laura Roslin

After Cally's funeral, Tigh and Tory discuss the positives and negatives of being Cylons. Tory wants to turn off guilt, but Tigh wants to keep his grief as a sign of humanity. Later Tory seduces Baltar again, as his cult's headquarters are attacked by a group opposing their monotheistic beliefs. Baltar urges his followers to retaliate against their attackers, The Sons of Ares. Baltar breaks into a polytheistic religious meeting, but is arrested before a riot can start. Tigh visits Caprica Six in the brig, but suffers a hallucination in which he sees her as Ellen. In response to the religious unrest, Roslin enacts an emergency decree outlawing meetings of more than twelve people.

After a near-fatal incident caused by Tyrol's distracted state of mind, he becomes angry when Adama tries to comfort him. He reveals his contempt of Cally and soon turns on the Admiral, provoking him to demote him. Roslin visits Baltar in the brig, warning him that as a dying woman, she's less likely to be troubled by the morality of her actions. When he is released, Baltar tries to return to his cult's headquarters, but is prevented by armed guards. Head Six urges him to be defiant, and it looks like he's about to be badly injured when Lee Adama arrives. The Quorum has overturned Roslin's emergency decree. In the Brig, Caprica Six first beats, then kisses Tigh, who responds. Later, Baltar begins to address his people, who listen in rapt attention.

'Escape Velocity', coming so early in the season, was one of the first episodes to give viewers an idea of just how bad things were going to get for each of our characters as the end drew ever closer. Still reeling from the revelations of their true natures, the final four Cylons struggle to get a handle on their new identities, while Roslin's determination to keep the fleet intact and alive brings her ever closer to an irredeemable political precipice. Baltar, meanwhile, seems to look into the abyss — and find his own version of God staring back. It's an episode depicting many role-reversals for our

Opposite: Adama and Roslin grow steadily closer as she battles her cancer for the second time.

main characters, and none of them ever truly returns to their former selves as a result. Particularly Saul Tigh and Caprica Six, who find themselves in a relationship that no one could have predicted prior to the end of season three.

"We knew it would be shocking," says writer Jane Espenson of the producers' decision to throw this relationship into the mix. "But we also saw the potential for something very sweet here. Tigh lost Ellen at his own hand, but he never stopped loving her. The idea that he could reclaim some kind of happiness that had an echo of his former relationship was very appealing. And Caprica has an amazing capacity for love... It sounded so unlikely at first, but once we started picturing it, it just seemed as if it might work. I was thrilled to get to write their first encounter."

Within that first encounter and also subsequent trysts between the two Cylons, however, there is of course a greater revelation that is first hinted at in 'Escape Velocity'. Saul's hallucinations of Ellen Tigh were the first time the audience had seen her in that context — and the first time the writers had firmly put into motion something that they had been planning for a while, namely the positioning of Ellen Tigh as the fabled fifth Cylon. "There was a point at which we drew a breath, and thought about whether or not we wanted to pull the trigger on that or leave ourselves open to other options," says Espenson. "Obviously, we did pull the trigger, and were very happy with the outcome."

For Tricia Helfer, the fact that she knew Tigh was seeing Ellen as well as Caprica Six during their encounters made working out the relationship between these two characters doubly difficult. "She was left really raw and open from her experiences with Baltar and fleeing the Baseship with Hera and just being in the brig," says Helfer. "She was very emotionally depleted, and then here comes this person who she's intrigued by, but doesn't know why. I didn't really know too much going into it about what was going to happen, and I certainly didn't know she was going to get pregnant when we filmed the first kiss. Once we realised that these characters were in a relationship, Michael Hogan and I had a few more discussions about, 'Is this just because he's seeing Ellen Tigh in visions?' That definitely complicated things a little. Is he falling in love with Caprica Six just because there's something about her that reminds him of Ellen?"

Another character with a crisis that comes to the fore in this episode was Chief Tyrol. Still shocked by the discovery of his true heritage and the death of his wife Cally, Galen really goes off at the deep end. The scenes depicting his rant about Cally are disturbing and resonate with despair. "I really wanted to say something about relationships in the fleet, for one thing," says Jane Espenson of those scenes. "People are undoubtedly faced with more limited choices than they would have had before humanity was nearly

SURVEILLANCE: ADDITIONAL

In the scene where Saul Tigh and Tyrol speak following Cally's funeral, the executive officer is clearly wearing Admiral pips on his jacket. In his podcast broadcast about the episode, Ron Moore joked that anyone cleverly paying attention to this would have either been given a sneaky signpost towards the identity of the final Cylon... or had discovered a wardrobe mistake. At the time, the identity of the final Cylon had yet to be revealed, so speculation was rampant. But the pips were, of course, a wardrobe error rather than anything with deeper meaning.

wiped out. And I wanted to point at the Chief's feelings for Boomer, which were, of course, undergoing some re-evaluation in his own mind. But I think there was also a sense in which he felt so guilty, and so genuinely grief-stricken that he wanted to say whatever it took to get some kind of slap-down from the Admiral — which he got. It's a complicated bundle of emotions and motivations, and I thought Aaron did it perfectly."

"I never had to tell Aaron anything about what his character was going through," laughs Edward James Olmos, who besides sharing those scenes with Aaron Douglas as an actor, was also directing the episode. "It was just the opposite, I really felt that everyone had such a good handle on their characters. I didn't have to ever worry where any of the characters were located. I was more into trying to bring a new passion and dimension to the directorial [aspects] of the piece. Each one of the characters is going through such difficult emotional instability that all you can do is just make sure you know where they are coming from, where they are and where they are going. So it's mainly studying past stories and reviewing and then preparing to go forward from there. You have to do your homework."

This episode also began Baltar's earnest interest and investigations into religion, although, as Espenson points out, whether it was actually a turning point for the character or not is a matter for debate. "I'm not sure even Baltar knows for sure," she says. "I think he believes in all of his turning points when they happen, but they do have a habit of melting away in the light of self-interest." ■

Above: The odd couple — Tigh cannot help being drawn to Six, still imprisoned in *Galactica's* brig.

SURVEILLANCE: ADDITIONAL

Aaron Douglas does an extremely good impression of Edward James Olmos, to the extent that if Olmos was away from set when a read-through had been scheduled, Douglas would stand in and read Olmos' lines. "It would be quite funny when Adama would have a scene with Tyrol," he told the Chief's Deck Livejournal community. "It was just me talking for two pages."

[THE ROAD LESS TRAVELLED]

WRITTEN BY: Mark Verheiden
DIRECTED BY: Michael Rymer

GUEST CAST: Callum Keith Rennie (Leoben Conoy), Bodie Olmos (Lieutenant Brenden 'Hotdog' Costanza), Keegan Connor Tracy (Jeanne), Alisen Down (Jean Barolay), Eileen Peddle (Gunnery Sergeant Erin Mathias), Finn R. Devitt (Nicky Tyrol), Leela Savasta (Tracey Anne), Laura Gilchrist (Paulla Schaffer), Ryan McDonell (Lieutenant Eammon 'Gonzo' Pike), Lori Triolo (Phoebe)

"In this war, people die, and it's just *stupid*." — Kara Thrace

The *Demetrius* is due to rendezvous with *Galactica*, but Kara is unwilling to abandon her search. During a Viper recon with Hot Dog, DRADIS picks up a Cylon Heavy Raider with Leoben Conoy aboard. He tells Kara it is time to complete her journey. Rather than destroying the Raider, Kara has it brought aboard *Demetrius*, and takes Leoben to her quarters. Anders, uncomfortable at their closeness, beats Leoben, but the Cylon reminds Sam that there is no resurrection for him, and, without Leoben, Kara will not find her destiny.

On *Galactica*, Tyrol obsesses over Cally's death, first remonstrating with Tigh and then attacking Baltar. Later, after destroying his own quarters, Tyrol breaks down and considers suicide himself.

Back on *Demetrius*, Leoben proposes an alliance between the rebel Cylons and the human fleet. The crew are vehemently against the idea, believing that Kara has been brainwashed by the Cylons. Helo tries to calm the tension, and Kara, overhearing, tells him to retrieve the Raider's nav computer. During the retrieval, the Raider explodes, killing Mathias. Starbuck accuses Leoben of doing it deliberately, but is still determined to complete the mission, which she sees as rendezvousing with the Basestar. The crew, angry and afraid, discuss mutiny…

'The Road Less Travelled' was an episode that changed significantly in at least one area due to a note from the network. Although studio and network interference is generally unwelcome (and where *Battlestar Galactica* is concerned, has usually been minimal) this time Ron Moore found the comments rather apposite. "In the first draft, we didn't have Helo over on the *Demetrius*," Moore explains in his podcast. "It was a network note that I thought was ultimately all to the good, which was to give Helo something a little more to do."

When the writers broke the story beyond their original outline, they discovered that this episode would be the perfect opportunity to involve Helo in more action. Choosing to make him Kara's executive officer on the *Demetrius* changed the structure of the

Opposite: One thing is clear: Anders, Cylon or not, will always protect his wife.

story, however. Originally, the plan had been for Gaeta to be the XO, and for the rising tide of dissent to originate from Athena instead. The writers realised this would be an interesting notion to explore — because despite the fact that Athena is herself a Cylon, they felt the crew would be inclined to trust her more than Starbuck, since they had no idea *what* she was.

Though it's true that Athena had made herself very much a part of the fleet, Grace Park reveals that, at least in her own mind, she never let the character get too comfortable. "She does seem integrated, but, for her, it's always in the back of her head — her Cylon status, how other people might perceive her, and the dangers and threats because of that. So though it's not necessarily been explored, I always kept that weighing on her. She's trying to be that model minority citizen, and she doesn't want to let anyone know her full power."

Another change in the structure of this episode involved turning it into a two-parter, with the action continuing into the following story, 'Faith'. Originally, 'The Road Less Travelled' would have ended with the scuffle that saw Gaeta being shot in the leg. Instead, this was moved into the teaser of 'Faith', which meant the writers had more room to let the story breathe.

One of the aspects of the story that was reinstated as a result of the episode being made into a two-parter was the interaction between Tyrol and Baltar, which brews throughout and culminates in a strange kind of resolution between the two men. An early draft of the script had even more following of Tyrol's obsession with investigating Cally's death. Realising that she would not have been able to 'space' herself, Tyrol set himself the task of discovering the truth. Though this was largely dropped, the episode does feature Tyrol confronting and then forgiving Baltar.

The final scene between Aaron Douglas and James Callis, though, caused considerable controversy on set. The shooting script went to the floor with both characters delivering dialogue. However, on the day, Douglas and Callis decided that they wanted to shoot it as it ended up in the final cut — with Tyrol remaining silent as Baltar speaks.

Moore, who wasn't on set that day but was down in Los Angeles, received a call from director Michael Rymer, explaining what the actors wanted to do. "I kind of pitched a fit," Moore confesses, "and said, 'No, you can't do this. You're going to do it as written.'"

Rymer, finding a middle way, decided to shoot both versions. No more was said until weeks later, when Moore was due to give notes on the edit in post production. "I saw it in the editing bay, and, as I watched both versions play, I decided that the version that the actors wanted was the correct one," Moore explains. He doesn't regret his outburst, however, describing it as a genuine creative clash, the sort that is bound to happen when everyone involved in the production is so committed to producing the best material possible. After all, as he points out, there aren't many actors that would have been willing to give themselves fewer lines for the betterment of the piece, as Aaron Douglas did for this scene. "I watched their version and it was better," says Moore, simply. "So that's the version that we used."

There were other changes that occurred in post production, as a result of time constraints and other concerns. One of those involved the death of Mathias as she examines Leoben's Heavy Raider. "The Mathias death scene was originally a bit more involved," writer Mark Verheiden told CoMix. In fact, when director Michael Rymer read the scene culminating in Mathias' death, he saw the opportunity to revisit something he had first attempted way back in the *Battlestar Galactica* Miniseries.

Above: Leoben Conoy (Callum Keith Rennie) encourages Kara's spiralling obsession with Earth.

"We hadn't seen a really good death in space," laughs Gary Hutzel. "Originally in the Miniseries, we had a sequence where one of the characters is killed while they're fixing a leak around the museum glass. It was a very elaborate sequence, and we shot all night long on that — we had guys on wires, in space suits… it was a huge deal. It was eventually cut from the show, both for time and because of the cost of doing the visual effects for it. So I think he [Rymer] thought about that and said, 'You know, we should have a really good death in space!'"

Excited by the idea of being able to send Mathias, who had become a semi-regular character, out with a bang, Hutzel and his team spent some time working out the scene. "She was going to do the whole deal of moving over to the ship, latching on and moving along it and everything that happens on the side of the ship," he explains. "It was going for a very protracted, slow-moving, *2001*-feeling space walk that ends in a sudden, shocking death to help punctuate that. But when Ron came in, there were hard choices to be made. I think he liked the sequence, but, as always, there was much more acting and storytelling than would fit into the forty-two minutes. Stuff had to be trimmed down."

The space walk wasn't the only material "trimmed down" for the final cut, as writer Verheiden told readers of the CoMix website. "There were, for instance, a couple of Helo/Athena scenes that dealt with Athena's feelings about the mission, and the fact that she feels truly accepted by the others on the crew," he notes. "This is followed by her and Helo's wariness/sadness when Pike starts making anti-Cylon comments, and all the old suspicions come back. I think those moments would have softened what now feels like some pretty cranky interludes between her and Helo." ∎

[FAITH]

WRITTEN BY: Seamus Kevin Fahey
DIRECTED BY: Michael Nankin

GUEST CAST: Callum Keith Rennie (Leoben Conoy), Donnelly Rhodes (Dr. Cottle), Bodie Olmos (Lieutenant Brenden 'Hotdog' Costanza), Alisen Down (Jean Barolay), Tiffany Lyndall-Knight (The Hybrid), Jennifer Halley (Ensign Diana 'Hardball' Seelix), Nana Visitor (Emily Kowalski), Alana Husband (Nurse Sashon)

"You have to absorb her words. Allow them to caress your associative mind. Don't expect the fate of two great races to be delivered easily."
— Leoben Conoy

The situation on *Demetrius* deteriorates as the crew mutiny following Kara's decision to rendezvous with Leoben's Basestar. Anders shoots Felix Gaeta in the leg, and Kara, shocked, agrees to take a Raptor instead of the larger ship. If she, Anders and Athena do not return within fifteen hours, Helo will jump back to join the fleet.

On *Galactica*, Roslin meets Emily Kowalski, a fellow cancer patient in the final throes of her illness, who tells Roslin of a dream she had that made her consider Baltar's teachings more seriously.

The Raptor crew find Leoben's Basestar severely damaged following the battle with Cavil's forces. Once aboard, Athena determines that the Basestar's FTL is shot, but she can link it to the Raptor's in order to get it to the *Demetrius*. The fledgling alliance is immediately put under threat, however, when one of the Sixes recognises Barolay as the human that watched her copy die on Earth, and beats her to death. Natalie executes the Six — a blood-for-blood act indeed, since without the Resurrection Hub, no Cylon can return. The Hybrid must be disconnected before the Basestar can link to the Raptor. As she is taken offline, The Hybrid tells Kara that she is "the harbinger of death". She also mentions Three, which Natalie takes to mean D'Anna, who knows the faces of the final five and also the way to Earth. On *Demetrius*, the fifteen hours are up and a conflicted Helo prepares to jump back to the fleet...

"I gave the episode the title 'Faith' because that simple word and concept was at the heart of where we were at in the show, as an actual production and in the storytelling, I think," explains Seamus Kevin Fahey, the writer behind this episode. "The episode was all about faith on all levels."

'Faith' was Fahey's first full-length script for *Battlestar Galactica*, having spent previous years first as a writing assistant and then as a staff writer on the show. "There was

Opposite: Natalie Six — a rebel leader willing to do whatever it takes to achieve peace with the humans.

so much momentum in the series at that point," he recalls, of setting out to write the episode. "We all knew it was the last season, so there was this drive of not only tying the knots, finishing the story of *Battlestar Galactica*, but this added layer of high expectations in trying to knock every single episode out of the park. I loved that atmosphere. So, coming last in the batting order allowed me to see the earlier episodes piece together, and I think helped me to keep fresh eyes in how we all could continue to push the series forward. I worked closely with Mark Verheiden in keeping that in perspective, especially since his episode 'The Road Less Travelled' is basically a companion piece to 'Faith' in setting up the events of the *Demetrius* mission."

In fact, as discussed previously, certain scenes that had been penned for the previous episode ended up being moved into the opening of 'Faith', instead. Had the episode begun as the script had originally been written, the action would have opened in the chaos following Gaeta's shooting on the *Demetrius*. "There was a debate in the room about how horrific the wound would be," Fahey recalls. "I wanted Anders to blow his leg off!"

One of Fahey's favourite scenes in the finished episode was another rather bloody set up in which Lt. Barolay is beaten to death by a Six, who is herself then executed. The writers felt it was important to show that the alliance between the Cylons and humans was not going to be plain sailing.

"I have to give credit to David Weddle and Bradley Thompson on that," says Fahey. "They helped me with the rewrites as we went to production. We talked a good deal about the beginnings of the humans and Cylons working together. We wanted to avoid a cut and dry, 'Americans and Nazis have to put aside their differences for the common good' scenario. That was at play, but we wanted to dig deeper and add more than just an 'us vs. them' conflict. And you just *know* there are going to be problems the second the humans step out of that Raptor on the Cylon Baseship. These people eviscerated the human race, and the Cylons, in turn, really see humanity as rubbish and didn't have a good time with the Resistance on New Caprica. The scene was also fighting the 'Barolay as a red shirt' concern. But because of all the issues at stake, I think everyone infused a lot of vitriol in where each side was coming from. There was discussion about how Barolay's death would play out. David and I kept referring to the way Jeff Bridges dies at the end of *Thunderbolt and Lightfoot*. He just has this look on his face and collapses in this field. It's just tragic and eerie and sudden; it really gets to you. So, in the page descriptions and on set during the shoot, we wanted to infuse as much meaning into her death as possible and give it all an impact. And, again with another

SURVEILLANCE: ADDITIONAL

The episode writer's interest with going the whole hog in blowing Gaeta's leg off was influenced by the question of who may have been directing the episode. "There was a rumour that Quentin Tarantino was interested in doing an episode and his schedule only allowed him to direct during the dates that 'Faith' would go into production," explains Fahey. "So, there was a small element of making it this bloody, awful, insane, Tim Roth squirming in the back of Mr. White's car-type teaser. It didn't work out, but I remember that being a germ of inspiration while working on those scenes. Director Michael Nankin did an amazing job with that sequence. It's so brutal. I loved it." Presumably if Tarantino had directed, someone would have also had to lose an ear...

film reference, I couldn't help but think about the end of *Seven* in regards to Anders wanting to kill Six in retribution. But the switch is that the Six understands (after talking to another Six model) that her sacrifice is necessary or all will be lost. For such limited screen time, I think it conveys a great deal about those characters and the series itself. And Tricia Helfer and Michael Trucco really went for it. They're both unbelievable in those scenes. Actually, I think in the script it wasn't an 'act out', but it just played so strong on film that we had to change it because their performances were so damn good. I loved that sequence."

The second thread to the script was Roslin's experience of meeting fellow cancer patient Emily Kowalski. Fahey reveals that this story evolved as a result of having to lose other material from the original episode outline. "Initially, aside from the *Demetrius* mission story, the *Galactica* side had a political story," Fahey

Above: Kara's nature is again brought into question, this time by The Cylon Hybrid.

reveals. "It was dealing with Lee's role in the Quorum considering Roslin's health was taking a turn for the worse. We had to lift all those scenes after earlier episodes were telling similar stories. I remember sitting down with Mark Verheiden one day and just talking about what other stories we could tell. It seemed like it was a good opportunity to tell something a little different, something to counter the action and intensity of the *Demetrius* story. I just kind of mentioned to Mark, 'Why doesn't Roslin start talking to other patients while she's in sickbay?' and right away it seemed to fit. Ron Moore sparked to the idea and we went from there."

Mary McDonnell also thought the inclusion of this plotline was perfect. "I loved doing it," she says. "I thought it was really wonderful, because it just allowed her to disconnect for a minute from being the President and being responsible for these people, and simply identify with a woman with cancer. You get to be just a human, and come to terms with the fact that your heart's growing cold. So I liked that, and I think it helped to launch Laura into the second half of season four, where she finally disengages from the job and allows love to steer her a bit. I think it set her up appropriately as a character." ∎

[GUESS WHAT'S COMING TO DINNER]

WRITTEN BY: Michael Angeli
DIRECTED BY: Wayne Rose

GUEST CAST: Richard Hatch (Tom Zarek), Callum Keith Rennie (Leoben Conoy), Donnelly Rhodes (Dr. Cottle), Bodie Olmos (Lieutenant Brenden 'Hotdog' Costanza), Tiffany Lyndall-Knight (The Hybrid), Brad Dryborough (Lieutenant Louis Hoshi), Leah Cairns (Lieutenant Margaret 'Racetrack' Edmonson), Colin Lawrence (Lieutenant Hamish 'Skulls' McCall), Jennifer Halley (Ensign Diana 'Hardball' Seelix), Colin Corrigan (Marine Allan Nowart), Andrew McIlroy (Jacob Cantrell), Judith Maxie (Picon Delegate), Iris Paluly (Speaking Delegate #2), Marilyn Norry (Reza Chronicles), Craig Veroni (LCPL Eduardo Maldonado), Lee Jeffery (Lieutenant Paolo 'Redwing' McKay), Iliana Gomez-Martinez (Hera Agathon)

> "To live meaningful lives, we must die — and not return."
>
> **— Natalie Six**

Kara knows that the *Demetrius* and the Basestar must arrive back at the fleet together, or *Galactica* will immediately attack the Basestar. Helo agrees, but *Demetrius* malfunctions during the jump and the Basestar appears in the middle of the fleet, alone. *Galactica* is about to attack when Tigh orders her to stand down, much to Adama's surprise. His order gives just enough time for the *Demetrius* to arrive, and for Helo to explain the situation to *Galactica*. As Adama's troops take control of the Baseship, Gaeta undergoes surgery to amputate his lower leg. Natalie comes aboard *Galactica* and explains the rebels' wish to find the 'final five', who they believe will help them find Earth. As a goodwill gesture, she reveals that they are amongst the human fleet. She will also take them to the Resurrection Hub, which controls every Cylon Resurrection Ship. Destroying the Hub essentially means the Cylon race will become mortal. It's also where the Three is being held, and D'Anna knows the identity of the final five.

Meanwhile, Kara tells Roslin what The Hybrid said about the dying leader knowing the meaning of the Opera House. Eager to learn more, Roslin insists on going to the Basestar herself, and takes Baltar with her as part of her dream. On *Galactica*, Athena is distressed to discover that Hera has been drawing hundreds of pictures of Six. When she sees Natalie talking to her child, Athena shoots and kills the rebel leader. On the Baseship, Roslin watches as The Hybrid is reconnected. It immediately panics, and jumps...

Opposite: Tigh surprises both himself and Admiral Adama by preventing Galactica's attack on the rebel Basestar.

For director Wayne Rose, the most challenging aspect of 'Guess What's Coming To Dinner' were the scenes in which Felix Gaeta lies in sickbay following the amputation of

his leg, singing. "We all knew that AJ could sing, he is an accomplished classical singer," says Rose of Alessandro Juliani. "But to do that in the context of the show without it coming across as cheesy or silly and to make it *real* — that was a challenge. Although in the end, it wasn't really much of a challenge at all because it really fell into place. But that was my biggest concern.

"Ron Moore knew that AJ could sing," continues the director. "And so I think at one of their writers' retreats, he said, 'We want to get this into the show.'"

The ballad came to be called 'Gaeta's Lament', and was written for the episode by Michael Angeli. "[Ron] wanted it to be sad, about a lost lover," Angeli explains at Bear McCreary's blog. "In a sense, we were creating a back-story through the song. So I wrote the lyrics with the lost lover in mind. But knowing how the show would end — with The Hybrid awakening — I wanted the lyrics to relate to that moment, as well."

"Michael's wife, Karen, who is a classical pianist, wrote the original score," says Rose. "Then Bear got hold of it and added his touches. I have the original with Karen playing the piano and Michael singing, which is awesome, but he'll never let me play it for anybody," he laughs.

For Bear McCreary, 'Guess What's Coming To Dinner' will forever hold a special place in his heart, as it was the first time he had been involved right from the earliest stages of a script. "The scoring process is generally the last step in the journey of completing an episode," McCreary explains. "I'm accustomed to writing music for a finished story. Here, I had the unique opportunity to help shape the musical identity before production even began. Writer Michael Angeli, director Wayne Rose and actor Alessandro Juliani and I all worked closely together to bring this song to the screen."

It wasn't just the way in which the song evolved that was unusual, either. To produce scenes such as this, usually what happens is that the actor will record the song in a studio prior to filming the sequence. Then, during filming, the song will be mimed to the playback of the song, rather than sung live on set. The levels of the song can then be adjusted in post production, and this also minimises the risk of extraneous noise interfering with the sound during filming. But for 'Guess What's Coming To Dinner', Alessandro Juliani sang the song live on set, and what was used in the final edit is exactly as you heard it recorded on the day.

"He sang it for real," Rose confirms. "We had the music, and we had it with him singing, so we could play it if we wanted to. We could have used some playback, like you do in a lot of situations, but we didn't. Sometimes we would just play a little bit of it so he could get the pitch and tone right in his head, but he did it for real. That was AJ singing. I'll tell you, when we shot it, it was amazing. It was one of

those magic moments on a film set; everybody was so transfixed by what he was doing."

"The entire staff got goose-bumps the first time we saw the dailies of AJ singing," agrees co-executive producer Mark Verheiden. "Michael Angeli's lyrics and Bear McCreary's music are perfect and it's such a nice touch."

'Guess What's Coming To Dinner' is another good example of how episodes of television so often change once they reach post production. In this case, Rose edited an entire sequence to add a series of scenes that had not been in the original script.

"The editor that I worked with on that was Julius Ramsay. I worked with him on 'Dirty Hands' as well, and we always put all the scenes [of an episode] on cards and pin them up on the wall. And we just make sure that that is the best sequence of events for the episode. Quite often, you end up changing scenes around, and we did that with that episode. We put the Opera House in, which wasn't in the script at all."

If shot as the script had described, the scene in which Hera runs through the corridors of *Galactica* would actually have been very different. "Originally, that was scripted as having happened in hangar bay," Rose recalls. "I argued to put it in the corridors, because the hangar bay is just a huge big open space. I thought it could be a lot more interesting to have them searching for her through the corridors. And then we could also mirror it with the search through the Opera House, which really worked out well. I was amazed by the girl that played Hera," the director adds, speaking of Iliana Gomez-Martinez, who took over the role for season four. "She was just so good. To have all those guys with guns marching down the corridors and everything else going on around her — she was amazing, she didn't bat an eyelash. We had another girl who played her in earlier season, who would just come on set and scream and howl. And this girl was the opposite, it was amazing."

"Iliana didn't care at all," agrees Grace Park. "She was having great fun — she had such a spark about her, and such a life in her eyes. With every child, they get shy when a lot of attention is on them, especially if there are fifty people around and everyone gets quiet and she's expected to do one thing... and it's something so simple — I think that shows a lot about human beings and what we're really like! But Iliana, she was a ball of energy and really quite adorable." ■

Above: Anders' actions aboard the *Demetrius* were the tipping point for Felix Gaeta.

WRITTEN BY: Michael Taylor
DIRECTED BY: Rod Hardy

GUEST CAST: Kate Vernon (Ellen Tigh), Richard Hatch (Tom Zarek), Mark Sheppard (Romo Lampkin), Donnelly Rhodes (Dr. Cottle), Leah Cairns (Lieutenant Margaret 'Racetrack' Edmonson), Colin Lawrence (Lieutenant Hamish 'Skulls' McCall), Iliana Gomez-Martinez (Hera Agathon), Donna Soares (Gemenon Delegate), Judith Maxie (Picon Delegate), Iris Paluly (Speaking Delegate #2), Ryan McDonell (Lieutenant Eammon 'Gonzo' Pike), Laara Sadiq (Priestess), Veena Sood (Quorum Delegate)

"And yet, that's what we do, isn't it? Hang on to hope in every hopelessly irrational way that we can." — Romo Lampkin

With Roslin gone, the Quorum needs a new acting president. Admiral Adama refuses to acknowledge Tom Zarek, and so Lee Adama asks Romo Lampkin to help him find a suitable replacement.

Adama orders Tigh to interrogate Caprica Six to find out what she knows about the Hub and where it's located. As he does so, a Raptor jumps into range. It's badly damaged and its pilot is dead, but Adama's copy of the *Searider Falcon* novel is aboard, confirming that it's the same ship Roslin and Baltar used to get to the Basestar. Using the last coordinates it jumped from, a recon mission discovers a destroyed Basestar, a Viper and what they think is the remains of the Hub. Adama refuses to believe that the debris is the Basestar that Roslin was aboard, and orders four Raptors to remain in place in case her Baseship returns. Adama then confronts Tigh, informing him that Caprica Six is pregnant — clearly his liaison with the captive has been about more than interrogations. He accuses Tigh of betraying him, and Tigh retorts that Adama's insistence on finding Roslin jeopardises the entire fleet. They fight. Later, Adama realises that Tigh is right. He can't continue to risk the entire fleet looking for Roslin.

Meanwhile, Lampkin determines that Lee Adama is the right candidate for acting president, and he is duly sworn in. Admiral Adama places the fleet under Tigh's command. Before they jump away, he boards a Raptor, determined to wait for Roslin to return…

"I have a thing about titles," confesses writer Michael Taylor. "I sometimes can't really get going on a script without a good title, because the title brings it into focus for me. And [with 'Sine Qua Non'], I was just thinking about necessities. The things we need, without which we can't go on, and what that meant, particularly in that episode for Adama."

The Latin term "sine qua non" was originally used in ancient legal documents to denote a condition without which something else was impossible. Without the presence of this one thing, this one stipulation, everything else is rendered meaningless... clearly an appropriate title when considering the events of the episode.

"Adama is coming to terms with that," says Taylor, "realising that he has been driven to take actions that he should know better than to be taking — putting the entire ship, the entire fleet, in danger out of love for this woman. And realising that there are many things he has sacrificed in this war — there are many things *all* our characters have sacrificed — but there's one thing more that he cannot sacrifice, that he *cannot* lose. He'll do anything to keep from losing that one thing, and it's Laura. I think in a similar way, Romo Lampkin — that cat was the one thing *he*

Above: Adama's realisation that he cannot live without Roslin is one of the most poignant moments of the series.

couldn't lose. The one thing he held onto, as much as he hated it, and that drove him to a kind of madness. So that's where that title came from. Without which, none."

The notion of sine qua non is also echoed in Lee and Romo's search for the perfect candidate to act as president in Roslin's absence. In turn, each of the possibilities is discounted for not having something indefinable and yet vital; until the only candidate left is Lee Adama himself. In fact, the thrust of both Lee and Romo's actions in this episode was the cause of much debate between the actors and the writers over the question of how manipulative Lee was in manoeuvring himself into the position of 'perfect candidate'.

"That was a bit of an issue for me with the writers," admits Jamie Bamber. "I thought it would be much more interesting if it *was* his goal. But they were reluctant to do that. The writers had some idea that Lee is good, and can't be doing stuff like that. But our show's all about the good and the bad and the bad and the good, and I think he *is* ambitious. He smells weakness in that episode, and I think he exploits it. So I made it, subconsciously, his goal. It is his goal, but I don't think he quite realises what his own ambition is. That's really what I was playing — a kind of conscious denial. He uses Lampkin to bring his thought process to the fore, but it's Lee's process, not Lampkin's."

Taylor argues that, in fact, he did see Lee as being consciously manipulative in the way he gained power as president — but not to quite the same degree as Bamber. "Jamie really thought that the character was even *more* ambitious than I realised," he recalls. "I had to think about that. We had such brilliant actors on that show, and sometimes when you'd written a script you'd been through so many drafts and so much toil to get to that point, that you didn't necessarily want to hear a whole other viewpoint," he laughs. "So sometimes with the actors it might seem that it was truly at odds with what you were trying to do — and then you realised that there was a point here. We had long discussions with both Mark Sheppard and Jamie Bamber about each of their characters, because they both had very strong opinions about how they should be acting, and what their motivations were, to make those scenes work. I had to go back to the drawing board a little bit and think, 'You know what, there's a lot right in what they're saying.'"

As Taylor rethought a little of Lee's motivations in 'Sine Qua Non', he realised that there was an avenue he could explore to make the character's journey more interesting. "The way I began to understand it was that yes, he *is* being manipulative, but he's not aware of it.

SURVEILLANCE: ADDITIONAL

Of course, one of the most powerful scenes in the episode is the showdown between William Adama and Saul Tigh. It's a confrontation that had been brewing for months. "I just love them and their relationship," says Michael Taylor. "There's so much emotion and, as it often is, the closest of friends can have the biggest fights. The betrayal seems like the greatest of betrayals, so I kind of just let them go! There are some wonderful moments in those scenes with them. It was on the boil for so long, and, what the hell, just let it out. It was very easy for me to write both Adama and Saul Tigh. Somehow they were both very real characters. They are both such wonderful actors, of course, and the relationship felt so real. So this explosion was coming, and in the end I just let it happen."

His ambition is guiding him. At the same time, that ambition, as it is with a lot of great politicians, is also alloyed to a genuine desire to do good; to change things for the better. And that really brought his character and that show into focus."

This way of looking at Lee's actions also mirrored what viewers had already seen of *Battlestar Galactica*'s tense political situation throughout the season, and, perhaps more significantly, how Lee is not immune to it. After all, Roslin had continually strayed from true democracy in an effort to do what she honestly believed would save the human race. And now here is Lee Adama, who was previously so interested in preserving democracy in its true form, effectively doing the same in order to place himself in a position of power — albeit for the best reasons.

"We all thought that Lee in a way is guiding that process, without him even realising," adds Taylor, "and Romo, seemingly in his madness, knew it all along — even from the beginning. From the moment Lee sat down with him, he knew where this was leading, and he was pushing against it all the time because, in his own mind, perhaps he understood where it would take him. He could not abide another do-gooder, another shot of false hope in the arm, because of where he was emotionally and mentally at that point. And he was afraid, unconsciously, what actions it would draw him to. Ultimately I really enjoyed that give and take with both Mark and Jamie. Both actors had really interesting ideas about their characters that helped make their journey that much more credible, and more interesting and subtle, for me." ■

Above: Both Jamie Bamber and Mark Sheppard had specific ways in which they wanted to address their characters' actions in this episode.

[THE HUB]

WRITTEN BY: Jane Espenson
DIRECTED BY: Paul Edwards

GUEST CAST: Lucy Lawless (D'Anna Biers), Callum Keith Rennie (Leoben Conoy), Donnelly Rhodes (Dr. Cottle), Lorena Gale (Elosha), Dean Stockwell (John Cavil), Bodie Olmos (Lieutenant Brenden 'Hotdog' Costanza), Tiffany Lyndall-Knight (The Hybrid), Jennifer Halley (Ensign Diana 'Hardball' Seelix), Colin Corrigan (Marine Allan Nowart) Ryan McDonell (Lieutenant Eammon 'Gonzo' Pike), Lee Jeffery (Lieutenant Paolo 'Redwing' McKay)

"About time." — William Adama

Aboard the Basestar, Roslin finds herself having vision-like experiences each time The Hybrid decides to jump. The Hybrid is panicking, jumping further and further away from the fleet, and one of the Eights realises that they are still heading for the Hub — the mission is still on. Roslin continues to see the dead Priestess, Elosha, during each jump, showing Roslin her deathbed as a distraught Bill Adama kisses her goodbye. Elosha tells her that she's become too detached from people.

Meanwhile, aboard the Hub, Cavil unboxes D'Anna, wanting her number to side with him in the civil war. Aboard Roslin's Baseship, The Hybrid senses the Three's reactivation. Helo and the Eight have planned how to attack the Hub, but although the Cylons plan to interview the Three alongside the humans, Roslin tells Helo he has to bring D'Anna to her alone. Roslin wants to know who the final five are first. The battle for the Hub is fierce and Baltar is badly wounded, but D'Anna is retrieved. Roslin finds Baltar, who, delirious, confesses that he gave the Cylons the defence codes that allowed them to attack the colonies. Roslin almost lets him die, but then changes her mind. Helo takes D'Anna to Roslin, but the Three refuses to give up the final five until they are back with the fleet — their identities are her only bargaining chip. The Basestar jumps back to the fleet's last coordinates, where Adama is waiting, and Roslin tells him she loves him...

The relationship between Laura Roslin and Bill Adama had been one of the most slowly evolving of the series. Who could have predicted that romance would blossom between them at the beginning of the show, when they seemed at such brutal odds?

"I'm pretty sure that it was not on Ron Moore's mind at the very beginning," laughs Mary McDonnell. "It was very natural, it was never pushed. And what I loved about it was that I felt it was a mature, middle-aged relationship. I don't think we see many of those that are truthful."

Opposite: Helo was a character that the network specifically wanted to be more involved in season four.

"I thought it was probably one of the sweetest and strongest adult relationships I've seen on television for a long, long time," agrees Edward James Olmos. "It was very well constructed; it had had the time to really experience what it was to go through this situation together."

In actual fact, according to Moore, the idea of a romantic attachment between Adama and Roslin *was* something he had considered at the very beginning. It was not, however, something that he wanted to actively explore at first. "At the outset, it was kind of obvious that they were a potential pairing, because they're both of a similar age, they're both of a similar power position, and they're in contact with each other right from the beginning," says the executive producer. "So right from the get go, you're saying, 'Well, I wonder if they're going to get together?' I definitely wanted to hold that off, and didn't want to go there very quickly. We just wanted to see how the characters were going to play out — they were in deep conflict, initially, and I kept the conflict going for quite a while. But the chemistry between the actors also told you that they liked each other at a certain level, and respected each other. I just let it be at a slow boil and let it develop organically over the life of the show."

The power positions that caused most of the couple's early clashes came to be their strength as a team — and, for McDonnell, one of the reasons that the pair were so drawn to each other. "The fact is that leadership is a very lonely position, for men *and* women," she says, "and quite often it is the politics of the position that can disallow people to have companionship. So to have these two people who sometimes disagree vehemently, and still be able to understand that human experience is much bigger than our opinions or our actions — I really loved that feeling. And I loved that she was given the opportunity to give up her resistance to her death, to her heart. I loved that she got to do that, and I think it was through falling in love. Because had she not fallen in love with him, I'm not sure her death would have been as peaceful. It would have been really frightening to die with a closed heart, which is what she saw with Elosha."

SURVEILLANCE: ADDITIONAL

A significant chunk of action aboard the Baseship had to be edited for time, including more of an exploration of the relationship between Helo and the Eight who downloaded Athena's memories. "He was supposed to bond with the Sharon, then, at the moment at which he has to reveal that he's lied to her, she's shot dead by a Cavil who made it aboard the Basestar," reveals Espenson. "It was all about being judgemental — feeling superior to this lookalike Sharon who illegally downloaded Athena's memories, then gaining respect for her during the action, then realising he was the real heel when he had to betray her trust. And the whole time D'Anna was observing their interaction and narrating it. It was fun stuff, but way too long."

Roslin's experiences aboard the Basestar allowed the production to bring back a face that the audience hadn't seen since season two. The priestess Elosha, played by Lorena Gale, was killed off in 'Home Part 1', but prior to that had always been a confidante of the President. As such, it made sense that Laura's subconscious, searching for answers and a return to the spiritual equilibrium that she had previously enjoyed, would conjure the image of her old friend. "We love Elosha," says writer Jane Espenson. "Billy would also have been excellent as a character who might have served as Laura's moral tour guide, but Elosha was someone Laura already viewed as a mentor, so that made a lot of sense."

The visions that Roslin experienced during the jumps, says Espenson, were designed to pierce the pragmatism that been strangling her purer self since the events of the Miniseries. "They are what led her to save Baltar's life and they went right to the heart of what Adama has said about the human race," the writer explains. "It's not enough to survive. You have to earn the right to survive. Roslin has always been a very pragmatic character— willing to rig an election, willing to airlock Cylons. I wanted to give her a chance to think about the moral costs of those actions for her people. If Laura Roslin stops being able to temper her pragmatism with love, then we're in trouble."

The fact that Roslin does save Baltar's life — albeit after a long struggle with herself — is really a somewhat surprising turn of events.

Above: Several Eights appear in this episode, including an Eight who has downloaded Athena's memories and Boomer — the only Eight to side with Cavil.

It was he who gave the Cylons access to Earth's defences, he who let the human population be so oppressed on New Caprica. After all his sins, and with all her suspicions finally revealed to be true, it would not have been surprising for Roslin to let him die.

"When I first read it, I remember thinking that it was going to take some time to commit to, because I didn't quite know why she pulled back, on some level," says Mary McDonnell of that scene. "But I think that if Laura was to be a complete character, she had to become a 'bigger' human being than some of the moments that she had had. This man had been her nemesis, but he'd also done some very good things, including save her life. In a way, I think she just had the experience of how horrible it would be to have made your life about revenge, as opposed to making your life about reconciliation. You can end up dying for revenge, and with a lack of forgiveness in your heart, or you can give it up and let someone live. Or you can perhaps die yourself in that moment, but die with forgiveness in your heart."

For Espenson, Roslin's strength of character throughout 'The Hub' was a key element of what she wanted to explore with this story. "Roslin's strength is crucial," says the writer. "Even in the face of D'Anna's cruel joke about Laura being a Cylon, Roslin keeps it together. The physically weaker the character became, the more she had to will herself to be mentally strong, which is part of what Elosha was teaching her: you have to be strong without being hard." ■

SURVEILLANCE: ADDITIONAL

The bedside scene in which a tearful Adama bids Roslin a final loving goodbye and then slips his ring onto her finger was not in the script. "That was an Eddie ad lib," says Espenson. "We were all in puddles [of tears] by the monitor." The beat was so touching that not only was it kept in by the producers; it was also later repeated in the finale, after Roslin's actual death.

[REVELATIONS]

WRITTEN BY: Bradley Thompson and David Weddle
DIRECTED BY: Michael Rymer

GUEST CAST: Lucy Lawless (D'Anna Biers), Callum Keith Rennie (Leoben Conoy), Bodie Olmos (Lieutenant Brenden 'Hotdog' Costanza), Keegan Connor Tracy (Jeanne), Brad Dryborough (Lieutenant Louis Hoshi), Vincent Gale (Chief Peter Laird), Don Thompson (Specialist 3rd Class Anthony Figurski), Iliana Gomez-Martinez (Hera Agathon), Laura Gilchrist (Paulla Schaffer), Heather Doerksen (Sergeant Brandy Harder), Finn R. Devitt (Nicky Tyrol), Sonja Bennett (Specialist 2nd Class Marcie Brasko), Barry Nerling (Adama's Corporal), Ryan McDonell (Lieutenant Eammon 'Gonzo' Pike)

"What are you waiting for, Apollo? Do it." — Saul Tigh

Aboard the rebel Basestar, D'Anna and her fellow Cylons decide to take Roslin and the Colonial troops hostage as bargaining chips in order to obtain the final five once they are revealed in the fleet. Adama reluctantly prepares to return to *Galactica* without Roslin, who, out of the Cylons' earshot, tells him to blow up the Basestar if the negotiations don't work.

When Tory reveals herself, D'Anna changes her mind about asking the final five to reveal themselves willingly and begins executing hostages, demanding *Galactica* deliver the rest and moving the Basestar into the fleet to prevent *Galactica* from launching an attack. Tigh reveals himself to a grief-stricken Adama, and also gives up Tyrol and Anders. Acting President Lee Adama puts all three in an airlock, threatening to space them all if D'Anna does not stand down. Kara, who has been taking another look at the Viper she returned from Earth in, finds a hidden signal that she believes is emanating from the planet. Stopping Lee from executing the Cylons, they persuade the Cylons that it's worth forming an alliance to follow the signal. The planet is there, just as Starbuck predicted, and joy breaks out amongst the fleet. But when several Raptors with both humans and Cylons aboard land on the planet, all they find is an unliveable world devastated by nuclear warfare.

The director charged with revealing the final, shocking truth about Earth was *Battlestar* veteran Michael Rymer. Rymer confesses that when he first read the script, so crammed with action and emotion, he wondered just how he was going to pull it off in the time allowed. "When I got the script, and it was [written by] David [Weddle] and Bradley [Thompson], who are very collaborative and pleasant, I said, 'Jeez, there's a lot of stuff happening at the end of this script. We have a stand off

Opposite: The revelation that Anders is in fact a Cylon introduced even more conflict into his relationship with Kara Thrace.

62 BATTLESTAR GALACTICA

and then we have the end of the Cylon/human conflict, and then we find Earth, and it all happens in the space of ten pages,'" he laughs. "And they said, 'Oh yeah, we know. We've talked to Ron about that and Ron really wants to go for it.' So I said to myself many times, 'Okay, I'm going to have to do a real number here to pull this off...' A lot of it had to do with creating enough psychological space between the beats, in terms of the way shots began and were revealed and developed. That was something a little more structured, planned and manipulated than I was used to doing on the show, where we were always very loose and trying to find new behavioural stuff that wasn't in the script."

One of the most memorable scenes in the episode is the moment in which Adama, having found out that his most beloved companion, Saul Tigh, is a Cylon, breaks down completely. It's a powerful, heart-breaking scene, and another *tour de force* of acting from Edward James Olmos. "Eddie just went for it," Rymer recalls. "The wonderful thing about Eddie, and the thing I think that makes it really work, is the vulnerability that he brings to it. It always amazed me how lacking in self-consciousness or vanity Eddie was. Eddie didn't mind going to pathetic. So many actors are a little bit self-conscious — they'll watch themselves going there and they'll go, 'Oh, you know, I don't feel comfortable being seen that way,' and they'll edit themselves. Eddie was literally dribbling like a baby in that scene."

Opposite: Role reversal: the son comforts his distraught father. One of Edward James Olmos' most explosive scenes of the year.

SURVEILLANCE: ADDITIONAL

The 'SNAFU' mentioned by Rymer and responsible for holding up shooting was the fact that the city ruins set had been destroyed by a storm. The biggest and most expensive location that had ever been built for *Battlestar Galactica*, the set was out at Centennial Beach in Tsawwassen, south of Vancouver. "We were scheduled to shoot it Wednesday, Thursday and Friday of a certain week, and it was assembled on the Friday before," explains Michael Nankin, who was due to shoot a large portion of 'Sometimes A Great Notion' amongst the ruins of Earth. "So it was trucked down and assembled on the beach on Friday, and it was magnificent. On Saturday DP Steve McNutt and I went down and we were looking at angles and where the sun was and planning our shots, and hoping that it would be overcast. And on the Monday before we started shooting it was a holiday, so I drove down because I needed some private time on the set to figure out my shots. And as I drove it was getting windier and windier, and rainier and rainier. By the time I got to the beach, the rain was being blown horizontally, and I couldn't see the beach from the parking lot. The first thing I saw was the art department, looking like that Edward Munch painting, The Scream, because the set was being blown to pieces. The set looked like packing material — there were pieces being blown down the beach, and the art department guys were chasing them, trying to save all the pieces. They reassembled as much of it as they could, and by Wednesday morning ninety per cent of it was there. But ninety per cent of ruins pretty much looks like 100 per cent of ruins!"

Rymer confesses that as a director he often finds scenes like that, with such heightened emotion, difficult to reconcile with his naturally reserved nature. "I'm Australian, a little bit English, a little bit reserved in my aesthetic. Eddie, with his strong Latin blood, loves drama, heightened, intense drama. With a breakdown like that, often I'm the guy dialling it back a bit, thinking that less is more. Obviously, this was one of those scenes where there was no way to do that. This had to be about the straw that broke Adama's back."

To balance the surfeit of emotion that the audience was feeling from the Admiral, Rymer concentrated on what was going on with Lee Adama. In that scene, his calm reserve tempered the thrashing waves of his father's guilt. "For me, the key to the scene was Lee," he says. "Lee becoming the father to his father, Lee showing strength and compassion. A lot of my thinking about a scene like that has to do more with a person reacting to this emotional storm

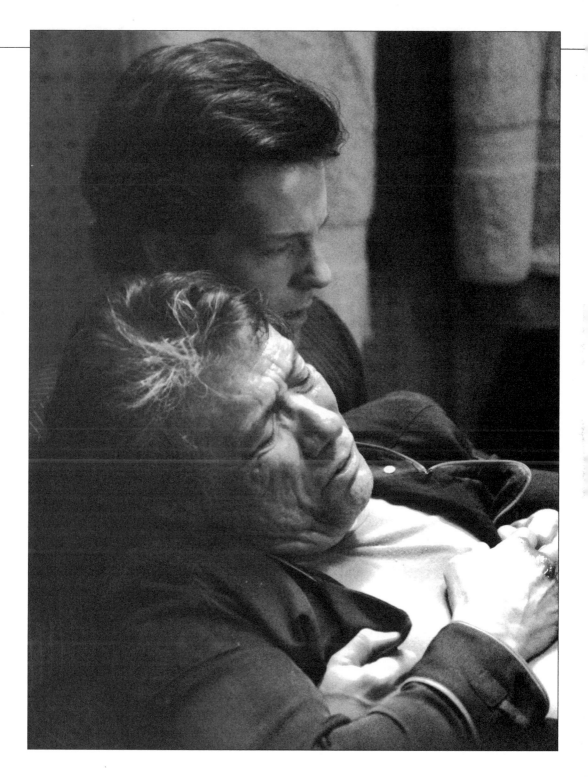

Above: The contrast of these two characters' evolutions — Kara, the pilot, and Lee, the pilot-turned-politician.

in front of them. And I think Jamie Bamber did some of his best acting [there]. One of the small revelations of the story is the intimacy that this father and son manage to create together."

Besides being a complicated script to shoot, both 'Revelations' and the following, linked, episode, 'Sometimes a Great Notion', were in prep when the 2008 writers' strike was preparing to go ahead. It was a time of great uncertainty on the *Battlestar Galactica* set, as no one was sure whether the series would last. If the strike had continued for too long, the studio and the network would probably have pulled the plug — meaning that either of these two very bleak episodes could have ended up being the series finale. And Rymer still had to find a way of making all the action of the last ten minutes work.

Knowing that the reveal of Earth as a wasteland could mark the final moment of *Battlestar Galactica*, Rymer decided that that final scene held the key. "I said 'The only way I can see this working is as a one-er. It has to be a big, long deliberate reveal, and the reveal has to be so profound that the emotion of it trumps any intellectual issue that might come up.' And that's tricky, because it's a television show of forty-two minutes and thirty seconds, and that's a three-minute shot. That's a very long shot in television," he laughs. "So it took some balls to hold the line."

In the end, however, the producers agreed with Rymer's idea, to the extent that they dropped the dialogue that had been planned for that scene in favour of silence and reaction. And that ended up being the final scene shot by Rymer before the writers' strike closed production.

"The entire cast were very antsy and sort of uncomfortable because they didn't know if the show would ever come back," recalls Rymer. "There was a real heaviness in the scene — this whole journey had led to this moment. And it was this incredibly depressing, somewhat absurdist moment. 'This is why we fought to survive? This was our dream? What a farce, what a joke!' And at the time, emotionally, the cast were quite upset, very much like the characters arriving on this planet — 'We've worked so hard for so long, and this is going to be it?' Because we were also quite aware that we were shooting the end of the show — that one could end the show on 'Revelations'.

Above: Tory Foster (Rekha Sharma) was the final five member least shocked by the discovery of her Cylon nature.

"That was quite an amazing day," says Rymer, of shooting the beach scene. "Because there had been a SNAFU, and the cast had all had to get up at five am to be there at seven am, but we ended not being ready to shoot until one pm. So they sat around in their trailers all morning, basically drinking together. Because this was it, this was the fizzer, this was the end of the show; this was how it was going to end, with a whimper not a bang. And it's just so interesting that that's exactly what was going on in front of the camera."

Besides potentially being the final scene, Rymer had also set himself an extraordinary task, as the entire shot was one long pan. Within it, the actors all had to hit their marks exactly right. And there was a time issue. "We couldn't justify going to that beach location and setting up that set just to do one episode, so I had to do my finale shot after I'd finished shooting. I had to wait around for Michael Nankin to be shooting his episode. I think I got a window of two hours to shoot that shot — and you should have a day to figure that shot out! I think I got about six or seven takes before Harvey Frand pulled the plug and said, 'Sorry we have to go back to Nankin's show, or we're not going to make our day.' I sort of knew I had it, but when I yelled 'Cut', everyone laughed, because I said it with such regret. It was such a wimpy little 'Cut!' because I knew that might be the last time I ever got to say 'Cut' on a *Battlestar* set." ∎

[FACE OF THE ENEMY]

WRITTEN BY: Jane Espenson and Seamus Kevin Fahey
DIRECTED BY: Wayne Rose

CAST: Alessandro Juliani (Lieutenant Felix Gaeta), Grace Park (Number Eight), Jessica Harmon (Esrin), Brad Dryborough (Lieutenant Louis Hoshi), Leah Cairns (Lieutenant Margaret 'Racetrack' Edmonson), Michael Hogan (Colonel Saul Tigh)

"So we don't know where the fleet is, and if we did, we couldn't go there." — Esrin

---

Several days after the events of 'Revelations', Felix Gaeta finds himself aboard a Raptor with two Eights, two Raptor crewmen ('Easy' and 'Shark') and a mechanic (Brooks). When the Fleet executes an emergency jump, a mechanical error sends the Raptor out beyond the red line, where the ship's FTL drive won't function. Tensions rise when one of the Eights is electrocuted and it seems to be murder. As Gaeta's boyfriend, Hoshi, and Racetrack try to find the missing Raptor, flashbacks reveal that Gaeta had a relationship with one of the Eights back on New Caprica. She tricked him into giving her names of human Resistance fighters, whom she then had executed. On the Raptor, the Eight convinces Gaeta to help her connect to the FTL drive to work out what happened to the ship. Gaeta is horrified to discover she has murdered the other human passengers to preserve the Raptor's dwindling reserves of oxygen. She says it was necessary, and accuses him of being aware (and therefore complicit in) what she'd done back on New Caprica. Enraged, Gaeta stabs the Eight to death, and is attempting to kill himself with an overdose of morpha when Hoshi and Racetrack locate the Raptor. Returning to *Galactica*, Gaeta condemns the Cylon alliance, and foreshadows his imminent dissent with a message to Hoshi to "keep his head down".

Battlestar Galactica pioneered the idea of supplemental storytelling developed specifically for the web. Not only did this provide a perfect opportunity to explore themes that the writers were unable to fit into the series proper, but they also allowed the executive producers to give some of the support crew on the production more responsibility. "I always felt strongly about making sure that we used these webisodes as an opportunity to operate a 'farm league' for crafts people and talent," David Eick explains. "It was an opportunity to let other members of the staff and the crew dig into something meatier than maybe they would ordinarily get to do — your bit players get to be supporting roles and your supporting roles get to be your lead roles and your greener writers get to be showrunners."

'Face of the Enemy' was no different in this respect, handing writing assistant and staff writer Seamus Kevin Fahey his second opportunity to write his own scripts. "After I had written 'Faith', I was mostly working in the writers' room breaking the last half of the season," says Fahey. "All the episodes had been assigned, so I was honestly trying to figure out a way to do more writing."

Producer Jane Espenson offered to co-write, and together, under the supervision of Ron Moore, 'Face of the Enemy' was developed.

"At first we developed a story that carefully avoided established characters and that didn't touch any of the main *BSG* plotlines," Espenson recalls. "It was about a Raptor mission that went wrong, but it wasn't this story."

"The question was: when would these webisodes take place?" Fahey adds.

Below: Grace Park played two new incarnations of her Eight character in 'Face of the Enemy'.

"I started hammering out a couple of ideas around certain events. Going back to revisit New Caprica was always at the centre of it all. Ron heard some of the ideas, and really stressed that this was an opportunity to bridge the first half and the second half of season four, which I think was the right instinct. We all had been kicking around a kind of Alfred Hitchcock's *Lifeboat* story that would take place on a Raptor. So, once we made those choices, it started to click."

In using the webisodes to connect the two halves of the final season, the writers also realised that they could sew the seeds for one of the major events of the final episodes — Gaeta's armed uprising. "Ron was the one who said that we could make these webisodes really do some lifting for the series by helping bolster Gaeta's motivation for why he found it so necessary to resist combining forces with the Cylons," Espenson notes. "From that point on, we were building the story around Gaeta. That took us to one of the show's remaining open mysteries — what had Baltar whispered to Gaeta that one time? What had Gaeta done on New Caprica?"

Though they had the framework for the script, the two writers encountered plenty of complications as they actually tried to lock down the story. One significant aspect in casting Gaeta as the main character was the availability of Alessandro Juliani. The extended writers' strike meant that many of the actors they would have otherwise used were off doing other projects. Originally, for example, the webisodes would have featured Tricia Helfer as well as Grace Park, with Sixes as well as Eights playing a role.

"We wrote many, many versions of the script as the scheduling of the shoot and the availability of the actors changed," Espenson admits. "We had a version with two Sixes, with two Eights, with a Six and an Eight, and another one with two Eights in which the final three alive on the Raptor were Gaeta and both Eights. We had a version with Admiral Adama in it, and a version with the pilot Narcho. The actual cast wasn't settled until right before we started filming, so the script stayed very fluid — or maybe the word is fractured. It was a huge relief when we actually knew who we had."

"They had to shoot these at the same time as the two-part finale, so scheduling was complicated," Fahey adds. "I actually think that worked for the best. The idea that Cylons have models, and that we see an Eight killing another Eight, and Gaeta having these flashbacks with another Eight, fuels the theme: they are not human. Can they be trusted? Is this model trying to manipulate me/the humans? Can you have feelings for them? Etcetera."

Wayne Rose, who had also been a graduate of the "Webisode Farm League", having moved from second unit director to director for the first series of webisodes, 'The Resistance', once again took the helm for 'Face of the Enemy'. It was, he reports, a "crazy" shoot. "At the time, we were shooting the finale, which was a three-hour episode, and we were also planning the shooting of 'The Plan' DVD movie," he recalls. "We had major actor availability problems. We also had this huge Roland Emmerich movie, 2012, coming in and taking over our stage space and they wanted us out as soon as possible. So there was so much going on, and we kept saying to each other, 'They're never going to ask us to shoot webisodes. It's not going to happen.' We were just too busy."

Another very basic problem was that the Battlestar Galactica set was quite literally being torn down around the production's ears. The construction department was striking the set as soon as each component had wrapped filming for the finale, so actually being able to find somewhere still standing would be a very real problem if the network and studio decided it did actually want another series of webisodes. "We didn't have any stage space left. The minute they finished a scene and that set was done, they'd rip the lights out and come in and crunch it," Rose laughs. "We also had auction people there, and as we were shooting, we would finish with a prop or something and they would grab it, catalogue it for the auction, and it was gone!"

When the greenlight came through for 'Face of the Enemy', therefore, Rose, Fahey and Espenson had to adjust the script very quickly to accommodate what could actually be used. "Jane had written a scene in the CIC," says Rose. "Well, the CIC wasn't there any more. So we thought, 'What sets are still standing?' The plotting room! There was a photo team shooting digital stills of all the sets, so that if they want to do a web series down the line, they have these as references for virtual backgrounds. So even though they weren't *shooting* in the war room, the set was still up and it was lit. So we had a scene with Tigh and Hoshi and Gaeta in the war room."

As filming continued for the webisodes, so did shooting on the finale and 'The Plan'. Rose had a crew of about ten people (compared to a standard television crew of about 120-150), no equipment and very few sets. "We would steal anything we could from main unit," Rose laughs. "We'd steal one of their cameras, and if we couldn't we had to use a smaller camera, a Sony P2. We even used, as our second camera, a little Cannon hand-held that we bought for $800! We shot what we could when we could."

The webisodes actually hold the accolade of shooting the final ever scene on the *Battlestar Galactica* sets. With everything else wrapped — and the multi-million budget *2012* waiting to come in and take over — the crew was under immense pressure to get the last shots they needed. "The very last day, we shot the stuff in the tent," Rose reports, with another laugh. "It was such a pathetic way to go out: we had this tent inside our Baseship set, which was half torn down, and this Roland Emmerich movie — they were all standing outside, waiting for us to get out — so we were shooting like crazy. And we finally come outside this tent, and they've already started moving their stuff in. And there were two full-size animatronic giraffes sitting outside the tent! It was *so* surreal. Our last day of filming was literally this little tiny webisode crew of about ten, and Alessandro Juliani and Grace Park, in a tent in the Baseship with a couple of giraffes watching us!"

Despite the hectic, guerrilla methods that Rose and his team employed to shoot 'Face of the Enemy', the finished result is something they are all proud of. "I'm delighted with the finished series," says Jane Espenson. "Wayne Rose had to deal with a ridiculous variety of complications — I can't believe what a great job he did."

"Wayne Rose, AJ and Grace did an incredible job with such a limited budget and small time-frame to go on," agrees Seamus Fahey. "I'm very proud of them. It was cool to see that they were well-received — it actually won a Streamy for Best Writing for a Dramatic Web Series, and I think it was a great supplement to the final season."

"It was crazy that we managed to do it," Rose laughs, "but it was fun. It was as guerrilla as you can possibly get!" ■

[SOMETIMES A GREAT NOTION]

WRITTEN BY: Bradley Thompson and David Weddle
DIRECTED BY: Michael Nankin

GUEST CAST: Lucy Lawless (D'Anna Biers), Callum Keith Rennie (Leoben Conoy), Kate Vernon (Ellen Tigh), Brad Dryborough (Lieutenant Louis Hoshi), Don Thompson (Specialist 3rd Class Anthony Figurski), Iliana Gomez-Martinez (Hera Agathon), Sonja Bennett (Specialist 2nd Class Marcie Brasko)

> "Felix, please. I just want to hang on to this feeling for as long as I can."
> — Anastasia Dualla

Examinations of the remains found on Earth reveal that all its inhabitants were Cylon, not human. Adama does not reveal this to the human fleet. While exploring the ruined cities, Anders, Tyrol, Tory and Tigh all have visions of themselves before its demise. Kara finds the origin of the beacon that led her back to Earth, and discovers her own burned-out Viper, complete with a skeleton bearing her dogtags. Leoben, who accompanied her, has no explanation, and retreats, disturbed. Both the human fleet and the rebel Cylons descend into despair — Roslin burns her scriptures, and Adama tries to provoke Tigh into killing him. Lee Adama goes on a date with his estranged wife, Dee, who kisses him goodnight and then shoots herself in the head. Tigh persuades Adama that he has to get control of himself and be a leader once more. The Admiral promises to lead both the Cylons and the fleet to a new home, wherever it may be. D'Anna Biers, however, decides to remain on Earth to die. Tigh takes one more walk on the ruined planet, and experiences a vision of his life before its destruction... in which he also sees his dead wife Ellen, and he realises she is the final Cylon.

Battlestar Galactica never fails to cram a lot into its screen time. But 'Sometimes a Great Notion' features so many vital threads that it is breathtaking from start to finish. It resonates with a multitude of very real shocks — from Kara's discovery of her own corpse and Roslin's burning of her beloved scrolls of Pythia, to the final revelation of Ellen Tigh as the fifth Cylon.

By far the most monumental event of the episode, however, is the suicide of Anastasia Dualla, which signals the crew's descent into the frantic spiral that forms *Battlestar Galactica*'s final act. For Kandyse McClure, who had played Dualla since the earliest days of the Miniseries, realising that she wasn't going to make it to the end of the series was a sad prospect, and one for which she hadn't been prepared. "I read the script in the hair and make-up trailer and went, 'Oh... dear,'" says McClure, with a laugh. "They had mentioned some ideas that they had possibly had for her maybe a

Above: Had time and budget allowed, this scene would have segued into a flashback showing Anders playing a version of 'All Along the Watchtower' 2,000 years in the past.

year before, but nothing that they were really willing to be explicit to me about. I received a phone call from Ron Moore shortly after I read the script, and he said that they felt it was really an aspect of the story that they needed to tell, and they thought that it would be most powerful through the eyes of Dualla. Of course, I wanted to be there until the end — just to be around those people and to be there for those final moments."

The actress also admits that at first she didn't think suicide squared with Dee's personality. And her death is clearly a definite decision to end her life — there is no hesitation. It's not a cry for help. It's uncompromising, with no possibility of intervention.

"Dualla has always been the rock," McClure points out, citing her support of the despondent Lee Adama during his command of *Pegasus*. "She's always been the one that maintained the last glimmer of hope. So it did take me a little while to wrap my head around it and find a way that it would be plausible for her to make that decision."

To reconcile herself to her character's choice, McClure researched the mental state of those who had contemplated suicide, speaking to people who had thought about ending their lives in the past. Through those conversations, the actress was able to formulate her own idea as to why Dualla would take her own life. "I saw her wanting to have some measure of control over the next phase of her life, over the next step she was going to take," she explains, "and that was the only way she could. With so much breaking down around her, especially with the news of Earth being uninhabitable, she finally came to terms with [the fact] that there was nothing to look forward to. Earth was this last vestige of hope, and it was devastated. That's what I found with people I spoke to — a sense of peace and finality came to them once the decision was made. They felt like they could give more of themselves because they saw an end in sight, and it was actually a relief. They had this final measure of control in their lives: that their last moment was going to be under their own hand and exactly the way they wanted and not by accident, or by a decision that someone else has made. And since working on the material and actually shooting that episode, I get it. It is a necessary part of the story — it's a natural human reaction to the situation so hopeless. And I gave it as my last good-bye — I really gave it everything I had. I wanted to show how much I appreciated and loved being on the show, and being there and being that person."

"It's never a shock when someone gets killed off on *Battlestar Galactica*," admits Jamie Bamber, "because you kind of expect it. But the *way* it happened was horrible and shocking. Even to herself, I think. She's putting everyone in a good place, and then she destroys herself. For Lee, it couldn't get much worse. It's brutally shocking, and I thought Kandyse was great."

Filming the scene in which Dualla picks up her gun and shoots herself was, natural-ly, very challenging for McClure. The director therefore worked hard to set her at her ease. "Michael Nankin was exceptional. He really just gave me a wide berth," recalls the actress. "We'd worked together a couple of times before, and he just said to me, 'Take the space you need, take the time you need.' A lot of my favourite shots in that episode came out of him just letting the camera roll moments after or in between pieces of dia-logue or certain moments. And he really just directed the cameraman to work around me. There wasn't a lot of talking on set; there wasn't a lot of discussion between takes. It was about maintaining the moment. Those final moments where I take off my wed-ding ring and my dog tags — I had this feeling to strip myself of everything that ident-ified me with the world. Your name is no longer this, you are no longer this person's wife or this ranking officer… it just felt like a holding on to this feeling — and then I just took a breath and grabbed the gun."

"In that suicide scene, while she has that moment at the locker where she's saying goodbye to her pictures and taking her wedding ring off, Kandyse started humming this haunting little five-note melody that she just made up in the moment," explains Michael Nankin. "And I thought, 'Oh my god, she's humming what should be the score.' So I called Bear McCreary, and said, 'You have to watch the dailies and incorporate this.' So after we shot the scene, I took her aside just with a microphone and we recorded a whole bunch of her humming. And we sent that to Bear, and he made it into the theme of the episode. That melody is woven all the way through it. In the scene where Lee is standing over her dead body in the morgue, not only is that melody playing in the score, but you actually hear Kandyse humming it." ■

SURVEILLANCE: ADDITIONAL

In the scene where Tyrol flashes back to his life on Earth more than 2,000 years ago, the writers had originally planned to physically show the destruction of Earth. "What originally happened was that he's still in the market place, and buildings topple, people are staggering around and their flesh is burned off," Nankin explains. "It was a $250,000 page of script and the studio said, 'Well, this has got to go — there's just no way we can afford that.' So the writers were in the process of taking it out, and I sat down with them and said 'No, you need to flashback to something — let's not be absolutists. Let's find a way to have this idea in there because we will really hurt without the flashback.' We needed a sense of the reality of their past. So we had a meeting and I said, 'Look, give me two carts, a wall and a green screen. And then the visual effects guys can put the city where the green screen goes. Can I shoot that?' And that was within their budgetary means. So that's what we did."

You can compare what Nankin ended up shooting to the original page of script, reprinted below.

EXT. EARTH STREET CORNER - DAY — PAST

Tyrol stands in front of a brick apartment building in a tight urban neighborhood. Corner coffee shop. Art gallery. Smoke billows in the distance from the burning city beyond. Dust fills the air. PEOPLE stumble past, moving away from the smoke. A disoriented Tyrol whips his head around, trying to get his bearings. SERIES OF QUICK DETAIL SHOTS, A LANDSLIDE OF SENSATION...

...A MAN and A WOMAN stagger toward him, silhouetted against the smoke.
...A car explodes into flame in the middle of the street.
...The building's glass door blows out, spraying shards.
...Tyrol pulls several pieces from his bleeding face.
...Closer now, the man and the woman have smudged and scorched faces.
...A flaming phone pole crashes down, dragging its wires onto the pavement.
...THE WOMAN'S skin, where her clothing has torn away, is burned in the pattern of her dress.
WOMAN: Water. Please. Water.
They reach toward him. His eyes flash down at —
...their hands. LONG STRIPS OF BLOODY SKIN hang from them, like gloves turned inside out.
...Tyrol has to look away. At the doorway. Sees —
...A woman's black hair, her dark eyes looking out at him. Could it be Sharon? No. Before we can recognize her, she turns away from the shattered opening.
Tyrol suddenly runs toward the apartment entrance. The sky WHITES OUT with a stupendous ROAR as another NUKE detonates. FOR AN INSTANT...
Tyrol's eyes see HIS SHADOW on the brick, just as his body's swallowed in the WHITE LIGHT AND ROAR.

[A DISQUIET FOLLOWS MY SOUL]

WRITTEN BY: Ron Moore
DIRECTED BY: Ron Moore

GUEST CAST: Richard Hatch (Tom Zarek), Donnelly Rhodes (Dr. Cottleee, Bodie Olmos (Lieutenant Brenden 'Hotdog' Costanza), Keegan Connor Tracy (Jeanne), Kerry Norton (Medic Layne Ishay), Brad Dryborough (Lieutenant Louis Hoshi), Christina Schild (Playa Palacios), Biski Gugushe (Sekou Hamilton), Laura Gilchrist (Paulla Schaffer), Finn R. Devitt (Nicky Tyrol), Donna Soares (Speaking Delegate #1), Andrew McIlroy (Jacob Cantrell), Judith Maxie (Picon Delegate), Marilyn Norry (Reza Chronicles), Veena Sood (Quorum Delegate)

> "You know, there are days that I really hate this job."
> — **William Adama**

Tigh and Six are being checked by Doc Cottle. Six reminds Tigh that, previously, Cylon-Cylon couplings have not been fruitful, making their child a new hope for the Cylon race's continued survival. Meanwhile, Gaeta waits endlessly to be seen, complaining that the Cylons get better attention. As if to prove his point, Tyrol comes in with baby Nicky, who is very sick. Tyrol offers to donate blood, and Cottle is forced to reveal that Nicky is not his son — Cally had an affair with Hotdog.

Adama and Lee argue with Tom Zarek, who is vehemently opposed to an alliance with the Cylons. Later, Adama discusses upgrading the fleet's jump drives with Cylon technology, which will require all ships to have Cylons carry out the work. In return for these upgrades, the Cylons want to become official members of the fleet. Tensions begin to rise — Zarek and much of the fleet are opposed to this idea and to having Cylons aboard their ships. Adama is adamant that they will comply. Roslin abdicates her power, while elsewhere Baltar addresses his growing cult. Zarek encourages the fleet to repel the would-be Cylon boarders, and instructs the fleet's vital tylium ship to jump away. Adama throws Zarek in the brig and blackmails him into giving up the ship's coordinates. Later, Gaeta, intent on mutiny, visits Zarek in jail. He tells him they need a leader to make everything right, and asks if Zarek is that man. Zarek promises that he is.

The main thrust of 'A Disquiet Follows My Soul' is the events that bring together Felix Gaeta and Tom Zarek, and the fermentation of their ill-fated, attempted coup. As a result, the episode features the final cataclysmic build-up of the growing resentment of both characters. For Richard Hatch, there was a sense of inevitability in Zarek's actions, as the character felt there was no other path left available to him. From his point of view (and, as he says, that of at least half the civilian fleet) bringing the Cylons and their technology aboard was simply too dangerous. And yet his attempts to bring this into debate through democratic channels had failed, repeatedly. So, when Gaeta suggests a coup, says Hatch, it's not surprising Zarek is willing give his all.

"When he challenges them, he's put in prison," points out the actor. "So here's a man who has no recourse to say, 'What you're doing could kill us all.' From his point of view, he's just as right as Roslin and Adama, who say 'If we *don't* bring the Cylons in, we're going to die.' Zarek has spent four years trying to do it the political way, trying to have a voice in the government, and, every single time, Roslin has blocked him. She rigged the election, then the next time he becomes president, he has to turn it over again because they're going to kick him out, even though it's not morally or constitutionally acceptable. They offer him a one-way ticket that says 'Either take the vice presidentcy or you're out.' In every single case he's been blocked from government, and once he's vice president, he's made benign by Roslin, and he has no voice or ability to say or do anything."

Above: Richard Hatch believes that Tom Zarek was right to stand up to Adama and Roslin's continuing move away from democracy.

With this episode proving to be such an important turning point for Zarek, musician Bear McCreary took the opportunity to write a theme for the character. "Despite his character's prominence, I'd regrettably never had a worthy opportunity to write him his own theme," McCreary wrote on his blog. "His scenes have almost always focused on his impact on the people around him, and rarely dealt with his internal thoughts or motivations."

"Richard Hatch was a delight work with," Ron Moore told this episode's podcast audience. "Richard is, no lie, *the* most prepared actor in the world. He shows up at the table-read having memorised all his lines. He knows exactly what he's doing; he's really a pro. The man is a consummate professional."

The professionalism of the entire *Battlestar Galactica* cast and crew is something that Moore had first-hand experience of from a different point of view than usual during the production of 'A Disquiet Follows My Soul'. In fact, this episode is described by Moore as a "landmark" in his twenty-year career, for it was the first

Above: Adama's refusal to acknowledge Zarek's position as vice president convinced Zarek of his inability to instigate change through peaceful means.

time he had directed. "I wrote the episode specifically knowing that I was going to direct it," he explains, "and so I was able to put it within certain perimeters. I had scenes I wanted to shoot, scenes I thought I could tackle, and scenes that I was interested in."

Before filming, Moore took advice from certain members of the crew about how best to approach directing the episode. "I walked the sets on my own and carried with me a diagram of all the stages and sets and laid out camera positions and roughed in some ideas of blocking," Moore recalls. "I was a little nervous and wanted to be prepared. Steve McNutt had suggested I do that, and I found it very useful."

Some of the blocking had sprung to mind even as Moore had been writing the script — for example, the opening sequence of Adama's daily routine, and, later, Roslin's run through *Galactica*'s corridors. Of the latter, Moore reveals that originally, the jogging scene had not been intended to intercut with the images of Adama taking the phone call. In fact, in the script, Adama is not reacting to the

SURVEILLANCE: ADDITIONAL

The lines of poetry that Adama reads out during the opening sequence are from Emily Dickinson's 'There is a Languor of the Life'. It's inclusion was purely by chance — Moore had simply written that, as part of his morning routine, Adama would pull out a book randomly and read a passage from it. Edward Olmos happened to pick out Dickinson, and read the passage aloud on set. When they realised how appropriate the lines were, Moore opted to keep it in. This habit of Adama's was prompted by something that Moore used to do himself: While working on *Roswell*, the writer would get his assistant to print out a random poem and have it on his desk when he came in to start each day.

Above: Shortly following this final
exchange with Kara, Gaeta (Alessandro
Juliani) pushes the button on his ill-fated
insurrection.

news that Roslin is exerting herself at all. Originally, the call was to be from CIC, informing the Admiral that ten Vipers were out of action. Adama's angry reaction ("Motherfrakker!") was in response to this news, after which came a scene of him in the hangar bay, dressing-down the Chief. But when the episode ran long, Moore realised that the scenes could be truncated and melded, making the phone call about Adama's personal investment in Roslin's wellbeing. "This scene was very important to their relationship. He's willing to let the fleet go to hell, really, for Laura," says Moore, adding that watching Edward Olmos and Mary McDonnell play the scene was particularly touching. "It was emotional to watch them play it. It was affecting, and the crew was choked up."

It's this scene that leads to the later reveal of the couple in bed together, the first on-screen indication that they are now in a physical relationship. Ironically, the most difficult part of filming this scene was deciding exactly where the telephone should go. As viewers will know, there's actually a phone fixed to the wall above their heads. However, since Mary McDonnell was wearing a skull cap to simulate baldness, she couldn't move around very much, and lifting her head to replace the receiver would have spoiled the shot. "The actors will tell you that they believe the characters have been sleeping together for a while," Moore reveals, "that they slept together on New Caprica and various times [since]. I didn't see it that way. In my mind this is the first time. But it's really one of those things that's open to interpretation." ∎

SURVEILLANCE: ADDITIONAL

Felix Gaeta's line following his tense confrontation with Kara Thrace, "I guess a pity frak is out of the question" was an ad-lib by actor Alessandro Juliani. When he said it in the first take, the cast and crew fell about laughing. Ron Moore, however, liked the line, and so re-shot the scene, asking Juliani to deliver it again — without the laughter.

[THE OATH]

WRITTEN BY: Mark Verheiden
DIRECTED BY: John Dahl

GUEST CAST: Richard Hatch (Tom Zarek), Sebastian Spence (Lieutenant Noel 'Narcho' Allison), Bodie Olmos (Lieutenant Brenden 'Hotdog' Costanza), Ryan Robbins (Charlie Connor), Keegan Connor Tracy (Jeanne), Mike Dopud (Crewman Specialist Gage), Ty Olsson (Captain Aaron Kelly), Leah Cairns (Lieutenant Margaret 'Racetrack' Edmonson), Jennifer Halley (Ensign Diana 'Hardball' Seelix), Brad Dryborough (Lieutenant Louis Hoshi), Colin Lawrence (Lieutenant Hamish 'Skulls' McCall), Iliana Gomez-Martinez (Hera Agathon), Derek Delost (Crewman Specialist Vireem), Vincent Gale (Chief Peter Laird), Colin Corrigan (Marine Allan Nowart), Michael Leisen (Private Stewart Jaffee), Laura Gilchrist (Paulla Schaffer), Andrew McIlroy (Jacob Cantrell), Judith Maxie (Picon Delegate), Iris Paluly (Speaking Delegate #2), Marilyn Norry (Reza Chronicles), Craig Veroni (LCPL Eduardo Maldonado), Veena Sood (Quorum Delegate)

"If you do this, there will be no forgiveness. No amnesty."

— William Adama

Felix Gaeta breaks Tom Zarek out of *Galactica*'s brig and smuggles him aboard Colonial One, where Zarek tells Lee Adama that his father has let him go. Lee leaves for *Galactica* to demand an explanation, but arrives amid the start of Gaeta's planned uprising. Disabling communications throughout the ship, Gaeta's position in the CIC allows him to hide what's going on from Adama and Tigh. His plan is to overrun the rest of the ship before CIC has a chance to react. Kara Thrace realises what's happening, but can't get through to Adama to warn him. She and Lee team up to retrieve Roslin, who goes to Baltar, hoping to bring the fleet back into order by broadcasting from his radio. Anders, Helo, Athena and Hera are put in Caprica Six's cell, and Adama and Tigh are arrested in CIC. Tyrol meets up with Lee and Kara, and promises to get Roslin and Baltar off *Galactica* — and, if they can bring him the Admiral, he'll make sure Adama escapes too. Adama and Tigh escape their captors and meet up with Lee and Kara, who take them to the storage bay where Tyrol has a Raptor waiting to take them to the Basestar. Adama isn't planning to escape — he came to say goodbye to Roslin. As the Raptor leaves, Gaeta tries to have the Raptor destroyed, but Hotdog hesitates. As the Raptor reaches the Basestar, Tigh and Adama settle down to wait for their capture.

"When you decide to do a coup — when you decide that this *has* to be done — you don't do it half way," says Richard Hatch, recalling the events that sent Tom Zarek into his final act. "Zarek says to Gaeta 'If we do this, people are going to die. It is going to

get worse than you can ever imagine. Are you willing to do that?' He knew exactly what a coup entailed, and he was prepared to do it. Just like Cain, in his mind he was doing it for the greater good."

With 'The Oath' began one of the *Galactica*'s bloodiest periods to date, with the remaining human population pitting themselves against each other in a bitter conflict led by Felix Gaeta and veteran political activist Tom Zarek. It had been a long time coming, as Roslin and Adama's desperate attempts to keep the fleet together and alive forced them into what seemed (at least to the larger population) a risky alliance with the Cylon rebels.

"There were tremendous inner negotiations, constantly," says Mary McDonnell, when asked whether Roslin would concede that her political moves held at least some responsibility for the uprising. "I do think that those questions haunted her. If they

 Above: Chief Tyrol's loyalty to Adama comes as a surprise to Lee.

hadn't, we would have seen a very different character. The fear of being responsible for the end of the human race was always the driving force [for her], and I believe you can't be completely true to democracy if you have fear as your motivator. Democracy implies openness and the tools to overcome fear. It has a courage in it. And I think fear of survival is a very primal thing — and how does one learn to lead without fear mandating one's policy?"

The ambiguity of who is on the side of the right in this conflict was something that attracted writer Mark Verheiden during the development of this script. As he told Maureen Ryan at her *Chicago Tribune* blog, "What intrigued me when writing this episode was the idea that Gaeta and Zarek were, in fact, right. Looking at the situation from the outside, the alliance with the Cylons was crazy and dangerous... no one in authority was taking time to explain how this alliance was going to help the crew or the fleet. Gaeta's motivations were pure, he was trying to save the human race, and that's the real tragedy of the story."

The problem with Gaeta's "pure" intentions, of course, is that with them he carried a certain

SURVEILLANCE: ADDITIONAL ||||

Verheiden had originally intended for 'The Oath' to look back at Gaeta as he had appeared prior to his slow spiral towards this point. "The script for 'The Oath' included flashbacks to the original Miniseries at crucial moments, scenes that showed a very fresh-faced Gaeta with Adama," the writer explained to Maureen Ryan. "It was quite poignant reviewing those moments, all before the Cylon holocaust, and juxtaposing them with the strained Gaeta/Adama relationship in the show [here]. Ultimately we didn't use the flash-backs, but it helped me understand the depth of anger and betrayal that would erupt between Adama and Gaeta during the takeover."

naivety that eventually led to the coup's failure. Gaeta wanted change, and although he said that he was willing to do what was necessary, when it came down to it, his conscience intervened. Zarek had no such illusions — for him, this was war, and in war, people died.

"In their minds they were doing the right thing in order to protect the safety of the fleet. And if someone had to die in order to do that, they were willing to do that," Hatch explains. "The only problem is: Zarek has been to hell and back and has had people killed around him and has had to kill for his own survival. He's crossed that line before, and Gatea has not. Gaeta, once that coup was initiated, didn't have the wherewithal to follow through and do what needed to be done. He kept pulling back at every turn. He wanted to make it a political process; he wanted to turn the coup into something that could justify the action. The trouble was, in a coup, everybody who opposes you has to die, because otherwise the coup fails. People have to die in order to save people — that was the decision and the choice that was made. Zarek made that clear to Gaeta before they even started: 'This is what has to happen, and you have to be willing to do this — are you?' And he said, 'Yes'. He *said* it, but he wasn't willing to commit and follow through on that. For me, Tom Zarek had to realise that he had to put his humanity aside and this has to be done *if* we're going to succeed. If someone had to die, they had to die. So, whatever the cost, he had committed to making that decision."

"It's completely crazy," says Jamie Bamber, of Gaeta's attempt to wrest power from Adama. "Lee's involved in the whole decision-making process about involving Cylons, and he understands. He doesn't like Cylons — he *hates* them — but he's pragmatic. He's a pragmatist, and, while he comes across as idealistic, he takes all points on board. And he realises that *Galactica* is dying and they need the Cylons and he's right at the forefront of that."

What the events of 'The Oath' did mean for Lee Adama was a return to what Bamber describes as "the Butch and Sundance" elements of his relationship with Kara Thrace. Starbuck, after weeks of uncertainty, suddenly finds herself with a concrete purpose — helping Adama put down the rebellion — and she grabs it with both hands, pulling Lee along with her. "It was great," laughs Bamber, of filming those frenetic scenes. "Whilst I loved the whole lawyer and politician thing, it was nostalgic — it was like going back to where we started. Kara and he start running around the decks and clearing *Galactica* of all these turncoats. It was very refreshing and very simple."

"Probably the most fun was writing the scene where Kara confronts the guys holding Lee at the Raptor," agrees Verheiden. "I really wanted to see kick-ass Kara again, and Katee delivered." ■

SURVEILLANCE: ADDITIONAL

'The Oath' featured the first all-out firefight in CIC, and the production realised that *Galactica* would need to bear the scars of this encounter. Verheiden himself had a hand in deciding just where the damage would be seen. "You'd think this would be a very deliberate process where someone painstakingly drills holes," he notes, "but in fact it was a guy with an air gun shooting marbles at the glass, scoring it 'bullet hole' style. He started shooting and suddenly marbles were flying all over the place. When that was over, I went around to the glass partitions and told him to shoot 'em some more."

[BLOOD ON THE SCALES]

WRITTEN BY: Michael Angeli
DIRECTED BY: Wayne Rose

GUEST CAST: Richard Hatch (Tom Zarek), Callum Keith Rennie (Leoben Conoy), Mark Sheppard (Romo Lampkin), Sebastian Spence (Lieutenant Noel 'Narcho' Allison), Bodie Olmos (Lieutenant Brenden 'Hotdog' Costanza), Mike Dopud (Crewman Specialist Gage), Ty Olsson (Captain Aaron Kelly), Leah Cairns (Lieutenant Margaret 'Racetrack' Edmonson), Jennifer Halley (Ensign Diana 'Hardball' Seelix), Iliana Gomez-Martinez (Hera Agathon), Derek Delost (Crewman Specialist Vireem), Colin Corrigan (Marine Allan Nowart), Andrew McIlroy (Jacob Cantrell), Judith Maxie (Picon Delegate), Iris Paluly (Speaking Delegate Dahlia), Marilyn Norry (Reza Chronicles), Veena Sood (Quorum Delegate), Adrian Holmes (Specialist Parr)

"Who do you want to be? *Who do you want to be?*" — Laura Roslin

---

Zarek tells Gaeta that for their insurgence to be successful, Adama must be executed. Gaeta doesn't agree, and instead calls for a tribunal. Lampkin is persuaded to act as Adama's counsel, but the lawyer already knows it's a sham trial — Zarek has appointed himself judge and jury. Sure enough, Adama is condemned to death. Zarek tries to persuade the Quorum to follow him. They refuse, and, to Gaeta's horror, Zarek has them all executed. Meanwhile, Kara and Lee liberate Anders, Helo, Athena and Hera, along with Adama.

Aboard the Basestar, Roslin realises that she and the Cylons are a target, and they move the Basestar into the fleet for protection. The Cylons want to jump, but Roslin persuades them to stay. Now free, Adama and his team head for CIC, but Anders is shot in the neck. Kara stays with him, eventually enlisting Lampkin's help to get him to Doc Cottle. In CIC, Gaeta is still threatening the Basestar, and tells Roslin that the Admiral is dead. He tries to jump *Galactica*, but Tyrol has sabotaged the FTL drive. Gaeta realises the coup has failed, and when Adama arrives, CIC is quickly retaken. Zarek and Gaeta are executed by firing squad.

Battlestar Galactica has never shied away from the difficult questions that plague society, and the conclusion of this two-parter is no exception. But what was truly shocking about the attempted coup aboard *Galactica* is the man who facilitated the uprising: Felix Gaeta.

"It seemed like a natural outgrowth from where we had been with the character already," explains Ron Moore. "He had been in very compromised, difficult positions — on New Caprica where he was working with Baltar, yet trying to aid the insurgents, and then he was almost airlocked. So he had major grievances against the

Above: Butch and Sundance — together again!

Cylons, and against people that didn't trust him. And then he'd just gone through the whole experience on the *Demetrius* with Kara, and had taken a bullet there and lost a leg... It just felt like, when they started talking about bringing the Cylons into a formal alliance, and putting them on the Quorum, it felt right that Gaeta would be one of the people adamantly opposed to that idea. Here was a guy who is really set up to question the power structure."

The idea of the coup and showing the abject level of discontent existing in the fleet was also important, Moore says, to keep the audience connected to the larger reality of the human fleet. "The show primarily follows the people aboard *Galactica*, but theirs is a unique experience in the fleet," he points out. "I just felt that, given what these people had gone through, there would be a fair amount of people who did not agree with Laura and with Adama, and were really having serious issues with the idea of having any trust at all in the Cylons. Once they find Earth is destroyed, and Adama and Roslin go, 'Well, let's keep going. We'll find something — and, by the way, we're going to bring the Cylons into an alliance with us...' It just felt like there would be a fair amount of people in the fleet who would just say, 'You've got to be kidding me.' And that would be the moment that they would just rise up and say, 'No way.'"

Gaeta's ill-fated alliance with Tom Zarek spells disaster for both of them, but, although Felix's fate seems unexpected, Zarek's constant conflict with Roslin and Adama made his involvement and subsequent end somewhat expected. "It felt like Zarek should have a separate end, a separate tale than to get to Earth," says Moore.

"It just felt right that, whatever the conclusion to his story was, it should end a little earlier."

Richard Hatch, the actor behind Tom Zarek, has long been passionate about the character and his motives. For him, Zarek has never really had a chance to show his motives, which are far more benevolent than some may believe. "There's very little empathy or understanding for what his motivations might be," says Hatch. "Most people thought that he was always an opportunist and self-serving, and yet, if you look at all his actions over the course of the four seasons, everything he did was for a greater purpose. I never played him as a bad guy, I never *saw* him as a bad guy. And even after this I was able to truly find justifications for his actions. Although," he adds, "that didn't make it any easier to play some of those scenes."

The scene which Hatch really objected to featured Zarek's execution of the Quorum. In the original script, the scene featured the Quorum agreeing to support Zarek, and he still ordered their elimination. "I said, 'No, you can't do that — that can't be. These are the only friends, really, that Zarek has. They've supported him, they've believed in him, they've championed him, and the only way that he would be forced to have to take them out is if they would go against him.' So they changed that scene, because the writers and producers are very collaborative. With the Quorum going against me and disagreeing with the coup, I realised that now I'm in a situation where they're not on our side, and in a coup they're either with you or against you. The hardest decision he ever had to make was to take them out. But, again, there wasn't much context there to show that. He actually cared about these people."

"I know it was very hard for him to go out the way he did," says director Wayne Rose, of Richard Hatch's last episode of *Battlestar Galactica*. "He's been so attached to *Battlestar* for so long, he's so passionate about it, that it was very hard for him. He didn't want Tom Zarek to be the bad guy in the end — he wanted some real humanity in Tom Zarek. There were a lot of discussions, and we came to a middle ground where I think everyone was happy. I honestly think it was Richard's best performance ever. I think he was fantastic in the episode, because he was so passionate about it and because he put so much into it. If Richard said, 'I want to try this' or 'Let's do that again', we gave him that. It was a sad day when we shot the scene in the airlock — and we made sure that was his last scene. That was a powerful morning of filming."

Having to say goodbye to cast member Alessandro Juliani was particularly difficult. 'AJ', as he was known on set, had been a firm part of

SURVEILLANCE: ADDITIONAL

Scheduling the shoot for 'Blood on the Scales' was extremely challenging, since during the writers' strike hiatus, the actors were allowed to commit to other projects. This meant that many of them weren't in Vancouver when this episode was filmed. "AJ was performing in a play on Vancouver Island, so he used to fly back and forth every day, and we would only have him for a few hours," Wayne Rose recalls. "Tricia was in *Burn Notice* in Miami. Grace Park was shooting *The Cleaner* in LA and *The Border* in Toronto. Tahmoh was shooting *Dollhouse* in LA. Jamie Bamber and Mary were both at a convention in Germany. We had no actors!" he laughs. "We actually shot one scene with Mary and Tricia where we didn't even have them [on set together]. Mary flew in as Tricia flew out."

Above: A naive Gaeta tries to have Adama brought in front of a court of law.

the regular cast, and the producers were so determined to give him a good send off that when he suggested that there was a scene missing, they agreed. Rose recalls, "While we were prepping the episode, AJ came to us and said, 'You know, Gaeta and Baltar have had such a history, I just can't believe I don't have another scene with him.' He said, 'I've got to have another scene with James Callis.' And Ron was there on set at the time, because he was shooting his episode, and he said, 'Yeah, I think you're right.'"

This was how the scene came about between Baltar and Gaeta, just before his execution. The scene also served two other purposes: slowing down the action, because otherwise it would have gone straight from the retaking of CIC to the execution scene, and as a feint for the audience.

"It was such a full-on episode," says Rose, "and this was a chance to just reign it in and stop for a moment. And we shot it like that. It was great little breather, and a nice little misdirect for some people. You think Gaeta's going to get off. You're thinking he's going to get a free pass, but he doesn't. That was one of my favourite pieces — that was a magic morning, as well." ∎

SURVEILLANCE: ADDITIONAL

One of the director's favourite scenes in this episode is one that almost got cut before it even got into the shooting script. It features a fugitive Tyrol coming face to face with Kelly after crawling through *Galactica's* access tubes, trying to reach the FTL. "There was a lot of discussion about cutting that scene," says Rose. "It was probably the most logical one to cut, because it didn't further the story in a lot of ways; you could live without it. So that scene almost didn't get shot, and when we *did* shoot it, it was at the end of the day with very little time. We didn't have a set for it, so that's not even a proper set — we just had a hole in the wall and we pulled in a bunch of those wire cages, and we filmed through those. We shot that scene in twenty minutes, or something. It was scheduled at the end of the day, so that if we didn't get to it we could live without it. But, thank god, it was meant to be, because we got it."

[IN DEFENCE OF ZAREK]

> "The truth is, from everything I've read and from all the scripts I played, it was clear to me that Zarek's actions were always about making a positive difference, which is what his whole life was about."
>
> — Richard Hatch

O ne of the best *Battlestar Galactica* resources on the web is Maureen Ryan's excellent commentary on the series on her *Chicago Tribune* blog, 'The Watcher'. Ryan interviewed many of the show's makers and wrote about each episode as it aired, generating intense debate about every area of the series from viewers all over the world.

When 'Blood on the Scales' was shown, Ryan interviewed Michael Angeli about writing the episode. She also offered her own incisive thoughts on the story and the conclusion of the ill-fated coup, which included the comment that, "Despite everything, Gaeta is not a bad man. He's mistaken and misguided but not bad in the way that Zarek is bad (in that sense, he's the Shane to Zarek's Vic Mackey from *The Shield*. Both are culpable, but not in the same ways)… As for Zarek, he really just wanted power, and he had no illusions about how he'd get it or what he'd do with it once he had it. That's what motivated him — the Cylon alliance just provided the opportunity he'd been waiting for."

As usual, Ryan's post was followed by copious comments from her readers — including one from Richard Hatch himself. It's reprinted here, in full, as an illustration of the passion that *Battlestar Galactica* inspired in everyone who both watched and worked on the series. For an actor to take the time, unprompted, to write such an eloquent defence of his character is quite possibly unprecedented, and, as such, a remarkable tribute to the show's impact.

First, having played Zarek for the past four years I would like to say that never did I play this character as a villain, nor did I think he was one and I still feel that way. After paying the price of twenty-five years in prison for standing up for human rights and seeing both his family, friends and cohorts killed by a suppressive government on his home planet, he had every right to distrust the powers that be on *Galactica* that seemed to think that only they had the right to make decisions for the people.

And since Zarek was blocked illegally by Roslin and Adama at every turn, including from winning a fair election, he had to resort to any leverage he could gain to assert some kind of voice in what had become an almost dictatorial government run by Adama and Roslin, who looked with disdain upon the Council of the Twelve and did pretty much what they wanted without consensus of the people.

Below: Richard Hatch's passion for his character is a testament to the power of *Battlestar Galactica*.

And after four years, Zarek had basically only two suits and hardly any money and was the smart man he was from learning many lessons the hard way. Why would he want power for the sake of power? He experienced first hand what power could do on his home planet and how it could corrupt. The only reason he would want power, having been to hell and back, was to ensure that the people had a voice in their government.

Did everyone forget what democracy is about, or do we just shut our eyes when the government no longer listens to the democratically elected representatives of the people just because we love the characters? And by the way I love both these actors and the characters they play, too. The fact is they broke as many laws as they claim Zarek did.

The truth is, from everything I've read and from all the scripts I played, it was clear to me that Zarek's actions were always about making a positive difference, which is what his whole life was about. My god, he paid with twenty-five years in prison for it, and with his life. And, tell me, knowing what we know about the Cylons and their programming, how could anyone ever trust them again? Even the human Cylons themselves have no idea of what they're capable of doing because of their hidden programming.

Also, Zarek was far from perfect, but tell me how in hell could he have accomplished anything in an honest and straight-forward way when he was blocked in every way possible and his reputation tarnished by Adama so no one would trust him? Adama had all the power and the military behind him, so he had to resort to whoever and whatever he could use to have any voice at all.

Does anyone forget that Zarek was in solitary confinement on New Caprica because he didn't go along with Baltar's agenda? Is that the M.O. of a power hungry terrorist?

Did anyone ever read Zarek's back-story? Doesn't seem so. People only took what Adama said about him as God's truth, but if you really study his actions you would see that he never did anything that wasn't for the reason of supporting his idealistic vision of a true democracy where the government is accountable. And this government was definitely not accountable.

The government of Adama and Roslin, as much as we love these characters, broke every constitutional rule of law to stay in power and to assert their will. Regardless of their positive motivations, they had destroyed a true democracy on the *Galactica*. And yet Zarek is looked upon as the power-hungry bad guy because he was one of the few to stand up and challenge them.

And why? Because he believed that just because we have a 9-11-type holocaust, you don't shut your eyes and turn over your power to the government, because that's the surest way to lose your rights and what we as a people have fought many wars to protect. In my opinion, to say that Zarek wanted power only for the sake of power is absolutely wrong, and doesn't make any rational sense if you truly study this character's actions and words.

In truth Zarek, Adama and Roslin all wanted power for the same reasons — to make a positive difference. But Zarek still idealistically believed that the government should always be accountable to the people represented in this show by the Council of the Twelve.

In closing, it's so easy to just write off Zarek as another power-hungry terrorist, but, tell me, where in this four-year story arc did he ever do anything that supported that belief? His words, his feedback, his words of wisdom, his actions, were always in support of his agenda to make the government accountable, and the reason for that was because he had suffered as much as anyone under a government that operated without accountability. And I hate to say it, this seems to be the direction the present government on *Galactica* is heading. You're telling me that only Roslin or the Adama family including Apollo has the right to lead and no one can challenge them? That seemed to be the case here. Democracy is a fragile institution, and can easily be lost if we don't make our governments accountable, and for me this amazing series *BG* has truly explored this theme in a powerfully honest way.

I feel privileged to have been a part of this wonderful series and I truly loved playing Tom Zarek. One of the most flawed, complex and misunderstood characters I've ever played.

— Richard Hatch

[NO EXIT]

WRITTEN BY: Ryan Mottesheard
DIRECTED BY: Gwyneth
Horder-Payton

GUEST CAST: Kate Vernon (Ellen Tigh), Donnelly Rhodes (Dr. Cottle), Dean Stockwell (John Cavil), John Hodgman (Dr. Gerald), Kerry Norton (Medic Layne Ishay), Darcy Laurie (Dealino)

"I remember everything. Earth. Why we're here. Everything. I see everything." — Samuel Anders

board Cavil's Basestar, we catch up on what's been happening to Ellen since New Caprica. Following her death at the hands of Saul, she resurrects aboard the Basestar with Cavil. She tries to stop him chasing the human survivors, but he wants further revenge. Later, he tells her about the destruction of the Resurrection Hub, and wants to know how to rebuild it. Ellen tells him he needs all of the final five, but he does not believe her and plans to extract it from her brain by force. Concerned, Boomer helps Ellen escape.

Meanwhile, on *Galactica*, Tyrol discovers that the ship is falling apart. Adama reinstates him to Chief and orders him to find a way of repairing the damage, though he nixes a Cylon-made substance used aboard the Basestars.

Anders' injury has allowed him to access memories of his life as one of the final five, who were researchers into the ancient Cylon resurrection technology. It had been forgotten as the Thirteenth tribe learned to procreate as humans. They built a Resurrection Ship, and were re-birthed aboard it when nuclear war destroyed Earth. They went to the Twelve Colonies to warn humans against repeating their mistakes, but arrived during the first Cylon war. The five offered the Centurions resurrection technology if they ended the war.

With *Galactica* worsening, Adama relents. Cylon technology will have to save his beloved ship.

There has long been a saying that 'No one ever dies in science fiction' and that has been doubly true throughout *Battlestar Galactica*. But surely one of the most surprising turns of events was the revelation that the final Cylon was none other than Ellen Tigh. It was particularly surprising for actress Kate Vernon — though not, perhaps, for the reasons one might imagine.

"I had been in touch with Ron," Vernon explains. "I would call him saying, 'Hey, can I come back? Am I coming back in a dream sequence, or a fantasy sequence?' So it wasn't *completely* odd to get a phone call from Ron. What was bizarre was that I had called him, and was saying yet again, 'When is Ellen coming back to work?'"

Opposite: This episode reintroduces the troubled character of Boomer, played wonderfully by Grace Park.

Above: Katee Sackhoff says that her personal reaction to Michael Trucco's off-screen accident influenced the direction that Kara and Anders' on-screen relationship took in the second part of season four.

she laughs. "He stopped my sentence, and I thought 'Ooo, maybe I've gone too far! Maybe I should not be calling him any more...' But he said he'd just pitched a storyline to the network that featured my character heavily, and if it was green-lit I would be coming back to work quite a bit. I was completely stunned. I wasn't expecting that — I was just hoping to get into another episode. So he said he'd call me as soon as he found out, and that's all he said."

Now, at this point any actor involved with *Battlestar Galactica* would be forgiven for wondering whether this meant that something other than human blood was running through their character's veins. But not Kate Vernon — because that conversation, she reveals, had already been had. "I was not thinking of anything Cylonic," she laughs. "To me that was not even an option. The reason being that when I was doing my last episode [on New Caprica], Ron came up to me and said, 'I'm really sorry that it has gone this way.' And I asked, 'Is there any chance that I'm coming back at all? As a Cylon?'"

And he said, 'No. Absolutely not.' And I looked at him and said, 'Really? For sure?' And he said, 'No, you're not coming back as a Cylon. You'll come back in a couple of dream sequences or fantasy sequences, but no, you're not coming back as a Cylon.'"

It'd be easy to understand why an executive producer would want to keep such a huge revelation under wraps for as long as possible. But, in fact, Moore says, his statement was at the time completely genuine. "At that point, it was true," he says. "We hadn't even come to the idea of the final five."

Kate Vernon, meanwhile, was anxiously waiting to find out whether she really would be returning to *Battlestar Galactica*. "I got a call from Ron a week later," she recalls, "saying that the network had greenlit his idea and that I'm coming back. I was jumping up and down, totally excited — and *then* he tells me that I'm the fifth Cylon! It was like the world just came to a screeching halt! What? I had believed him — because I kept coming back in Saul's fantasies, so he was honouring what he said. So when he said I was coming back as the fifth Cylon, it was like, 'Are you messing with me?'" she laughs. "'Am I on *Candid Camera*? Am I being punked by Ashton Kutcher right now?' I did *not* believe him. I really thought he was messing with me. So he then explained the whole story arc, and it was phenomenal. It was the shock of my life."

Though a shock, it was a welcome one, and the actress calls the fact that both Ellen and Saul were part of the final five, "crazy, beautiful poetry".

The episode also gives the audience some insight into what's been happening to Boomer since she split from the rest of the Eights. The show's title, 'No Exit', perhaps most accurately describes the situation in which Boomer finds herself. Her decision to join Cavil was another path taken in an attempt to find a place for herself in the universe — and, since her efforts to fit in with the humans failed so spectacularly, it perhaps makes sense that Boomer now tries to get as far away from their influence as possible. "She committed herself, perhaps more than any other Cylon, to following Cavil's quest to become the most perfect machine possible," points out writer Ryan Mottesheard.

"Boomer is not a happy character at all," says Grace Park. "There are a lot of things in her life that she's decided to do that have driven her to an unhappy, tragic state. Boomer was really going for a different kind of experience in siding with Cavil. She's at odds with the people around her, but her struggle to be a part of something seems to drive her to make these decisions that do the exact opposite." ∎

SURVEILLANCE: ADDITIONAL

The majority of the scenes between Ellen and Cavil aboard the Basestar were written by Ron Moore, and had originally been intended for episode fourteen 'A Disquiet Follows My Soul'. That episode would have flashed from the *Galactica* back to Ellen's story to immediately fill in the blanks that had been established from the reveal of Ellen as the fifth Cylon in the previous episode, 'Sometimes a Great Notion'. Then Moore realised two things: that Ellen's story was too important and required its own A story arc, and that episode thirteen was already too weighty. Instead it was decided that those scenes would be lifted wholesale and put into 'No Exit'. Since episode seventeen had already been planned to include Anders' revelatory flashbacks, the addition of Ellen's flashbacks created the perfect complementary story thread that would finally culminate in her present-day escape from Cavil.

[DEADLOCK]

WRITTEN BY: Jane Espenson
DIRECTED BY: Robert Young

GUEST CAST: Kate Vernon (Ellen Tigh),Donnelly Rhodes (Dr. Cottle), Roark Critchlow (Slick) Bodie Olmos (Lieutenant Brenden 'Hotdog' Costanza), Keegan Connor Tracy, (Jeanne), Patrick Currie (Enzo), Brad Dryborough (Lieutenant Louis Hoshi), Laura Gilchrist (Paulla Schaffer), Rebecca Davis (Naia), Merwin Mondesir (Marine #1), Tammy Gillis (Marine #2), Patrick Gilmore (Rafferty)

"Oh my Gods. It's Ellen Tigh." — Laura Roslin

E llen and Boomer arrive onboard *Galactica*, and Boomer is immediately arrested. Ellen and Saul's first meeting results in them making love, after which they go to visit Anders, who is comatose after his brain surgery. The Cylons discuss the possibility of leaving the fleet now that Ellen has returned, especially considering Six's pregnancy. Ellen is shocked and angry that Six and Saul conceived — she was never able to, meaning that Saul must really love Six. A vote on whether to leave ends with Ellen having the deciding say, and she says she needs time to think.

Tyrol is still trying to save *Galactica*, and has teams of Cylons apply a polymer to the cracks in the ship. Ellen visits Six, and taunts her with the fact that she and Saul just had sex. She then calls another meeting, saying that she has decided the Cylons will leave the fleet, but Saul refuses. Ellen tells him he loves Adama and *Galactica* more than either she or Caprica Six. Caprica, distraught, begins to miscarry. Ellen, contrite, tells Saul that Caprica needs to know he really loves her — and she, Ellen, believes that he does. It doesn't help, and Caprica loses the baby, a boy that Saul calls 'Liam'.

The writer charged with penning Saul and Ellen's explosive reunion was season four writing and producing recruit Jane Espenson. Though Espenson hadn't been on staff when Ellen was originally aboard *Galactica*, she found writing for the character completely natural. "I love writing for Ellen, she's one of my favorites. She's a character who manages to be both extreme and — very recognisable," says Espenson. "We've all met Ellen Tighs: women with very high expectations of what the world owes them, but with a charm that keeps making you want to deliver it for them. I did some work on the episode that was immediately before this one, 'No Exit', and I was fascinated with the way in which returning to Saul returned her to her old self. It's a really fun relationship to write."

Above: The early stages of the Battlestar *Galactica's* demise.

For Ron Moore, it was important that Ellen's new perspective on life, as a Cylon, have a significant impact on her personality, something that he spoke at length about with Kate Vernon. "I remember talking to Kate directly about it and saying that, once she wakes up with the knowledge of who and what she is, she's full again," Moore explains. "She is who she's always been, and there's a maturity and a wisdom to her, a deeper insight into a lot of things in life that she didn't have before. But the Ellen that we have known before then was still part of who she was. She was still that character, and she was still capable of all the things that we had seen Ellen be capable of — she was still randy, she still drank, she still had a tempestuous relationship with her husband, she was still petty on some levels, she had jealousies and darknesses and rages. But now there's another aspect, a deeper insight, a greater intelligence and much greater degree of wisdom to level out those rough edges."

That Ellen is still the same character as the audience first knew is immediately evident from her reunion with Saul. There was never any doubt that another meeting between Saul and Ellen would culminate in sex — but this time, their passion for and anger at one another has an unintended victim, in the form of the pregnant Caprica Six.

"We did talk about whether she would have the child," reveals Ron Moore, of the Caprica Six pregnancy plot. "We were open to the question for quite a while. We said we'd just see how far we're going to go. It wasn't entirely clear at that point whether she would have delivered by the time they'd got to Earth at the very end, and we weren't sure where that would take us. It was going to have fairly significant repercussions if we had gone that way, so we just decided not to. We decided that she would miscarry."

"Ellen comes back to create peace and move forward with our mission, and just gets so tripped up," Kate Vernon explains. "She's still Ellen, even though she's come back with all this awareness, she's still a feeling person and has always been deeply in love with her husband. The thing I've always played with this is that it's a great love story between Ellen and Saul. And even though Ellen was a bit diabolical and a troublemaker, it's because she was in competition with Adama. Her husband had this bromance going on with Adama and the ship," laughs the actress, "and it's like, 'What about me? Where do *I* fit into this — aren't *we* married?' So she drank and she screwed around to get her husband's attention, but it was all just to get her man back from Adama. So her *huge* disappointment when she comes back is that she finally gets to be with her guy and she finds out this [with Caprica Six] is going on. And she surrenders. She just tried to surrender. She never meant to hurt Number Six or anything like that; it was all just to hurt Saul. Ellen isn't a mean-spirited person. She's been wounded by her husband and lacks judgement sometimes."

Another character battling with the old and new sides of their personality in this

episode is Gauis Baltar. Having initially indulged in the dubious benefits of being surrounded by female worshippers, Baltar begins to long for something more — namely, to make a physical difference instead of merely an ephemeral, spiritual one. His attempts to give to the poor backfire when The Sons of Ares attack and steal from the cult. Most interesting about this story thread, however, is that it was originally intended to segue into a plotline to be explored further in the season. Adama finally supplies Baltar's cult with weapons to defend themselves, which would have been revisited later on. "It kind of got squeezed out," Ron Moore admits of this plot thread. "We were going to do more with that. We liked the idea of *Galactica* being undermanned and under attack, especially after the mutiny. There would be sections of the ship that would be cordoned off, and sections of the ship that Adama didn't even control, but Baltar's group had a certain organisation. Giving them weapons to defend themselves and to provide security aboard the ship made a practical sort of sense. But ultimately it was just one of the ideas that got squeezed out by other plotlines as time went on." ■

[SOMEONE TO WATCH OVER ME]

WRITTEN BY: Bradley Thompson and David Weddle
DIRECTED BY: Michael Nankin

GUEST CAST: Kate Vernon (Ellen Tigh), Donnelly Rhodes (Dr. Cottle), Roark Critchlow (Slick), Bodie Olmos (Lieutenant Brenden 'Hotdog' Costanza), Brad Dryborough (Lieutenant Louis Hoshi), Iliana Gomez-Martinez (Hera Agathon), Sonja Bennett (Specialist 2nd Class Marcie Brasko), Darcy Laurie (Dealino), Erika-Shaye Gair (Young Kara), Patrick Gilmore (Rafferty), Cherilynn Fulbright (Dionne), Curtis Caravaggio (Nathanson), Ivan Cermak (Corporal D. Wallace), Torrance Coombs (Lance Corporal C. Sellers)

"Listen, you may feel like hell, but, sometimes, lost is where you need to be. Just because you don't know your direction doesn't mean you don't have one." — Slick

Kara, distressed over Anders' condition and suffering anxiety about her own nature following the discovery of her body on Earth, turns to drink even more heavily than before. Meanwhile Boomer is to be extradited to the Basestar, where she will face charges of treason for siding with Cavil. Desperate to escape what she knows will be a death penalty, she persuades Tyrol to help her escape.

Starbuck begins to argue with the piano player at Joe's Bar, but gradually warms to him. He's trying to compose a new song, and as he does so she talks to him about her father, who was also a piano player when she was a child. She begins to help with the composition, realising that it resembles a song from her childhood that she used to play with her father.

Boomer attacks and ties up Athena, posing as her to kidnap Hera. In the bar, Kara realises the notes she's playing are in the same sequence as a drawing Hera did for her — and as the song comes together, it becomes clear that it's also the song that reactivated Tigh, Tory, Tyrol and Anders. As she plays, the piano player disappears. Boomer escapes with Hera, leaving Tyrol distraught at her actions.

'Someone To Watch Over Me' formed a unique episode of *Battlestar Galactica*, centring around Kara's relationship with her father and the song that had haunted her — and the final four Cylons' — dreams.

"The first thing I knew when I read the script was that I had to have an actor who could play piano," recalls director Michael Nankin. "It's obvious when they're not actually playing. The audience is too smart, and I didn't want to have an episode where it was one shot of his face and another shot of his hands. I didn't want to have that element of artifice, because I felt it would detract from the drama. It would also break the style of

Opposite: Tyrol seemed destined for more pain and grief throughout season four.

the show, which involved a roaming camera. I wanted to be able to go from his face and Kara's face down to his hands and back up. I wanted to create something that was really happening on the stage, on the set, and just film it. So they were my marching orders from the first day."

Finding an actor who could play piano to a high level as well as perfectly portray Starbuck's dad was a tall order. "We only auditioned piano players who were also actors," says Nankin. "And in the auditions, they came prepared to play, and *then* act. And I said, 'No, you have to play *and* act.' An actor who has to concentrate on the technical aspects of a piano performance is doing something real in his performance, and it focuses him and it makes the performance more real, because he's forgetting about his lines and concentrating on his hands. It was magical. Everyone's performance came up because they didn't think about the acting, because they were playing."

This book looks more closely at how 'Someone To Watch Over Me' and its score came together in the next section. Nankin, however, is still in awe at the effort that musician Bear McCreary put into the episode. Take, for example, the extreme steps McCreary took to make sure the piano viewers see played on the set is actually the one heard on the final score. "That particular piano, by the time we got it up to the set, was terribly out of tune," Nankin recalls. "It was just a trashed piano. But it seemed right, so we left it alone. When you shoot live music and acting, with people talking at the same time as playing, you have great technical difficulty in post production, because you need the ability to separate those two elements, and you can't. If you raise [the volume] of the dialogue a little, you also raise the piano — you can't separate them. Since we so liked the sound of *that* piano in *that* space, he wanted to include that not only in the scene but also in his score. What Bear did to solve that problem, and to give himself more creative control, was spend I don't know how many hours with a recording engineer. They took digital samples of every key on that piano, with different attacks, so that he could go back to LA and, with a synthesiser, program the sound of *that* piano on *that* stage into his computer and actually play that piano. So you hear that piano all through the score, and it's Bear on his computer, playing that virtual piano. He actually went through and replaced, frame by frame, every note that's played in that episode. And that's a gigantic job."

The episode also features the act that will later precipitate the end of *Galactica*'s path — namely, Boomer's kidnap of Hera. The scene in which Helo is seduced by Boomer as the beaten and traumatised Athena looks on changed considerably prior to shooting, at Nankin's request.

"It wasn't in the script," he explains. "There was a kiss and they sort of made out, and Athena

SURVEILLANCE: ADDITIONAL

As the production began the casting process for an actor to play Starbuck's father, they realised that they needed a performer who could not only act, but was also an accomplished musician. That's not a small thing to ask, and at one point, the production thought they might have a solution — get musician Bear McCreary to play the part himself! McCreary agreed to audition. "I thought, he's about the right age, he's a good looking guy, he'll look good on camera, and he can play," laughs director Michael Nankin. "Why not?"

During the audition, however, it was mutually decided that music was where McCreary's considerable talents lay! "For the good of the show, and of humanity in general," McCreary jokes on his blog, "I didn't get the role…"

didn't witness it. I read that and called Ron and said, 'How can you go down this road and not go *all* the way down this road? This is the one that everyone will be talking about — a woman watches her husband have sex with herself, with her genetic double. The internet will be buzzing with that one!' And the network was worried that women would be angry that a man wouldn't know the difference between his Cylon wife and another Cylon. Our response, was no, women will not be angry — they'll elbow their husbands and say, 'That's exactly what you guys are like!' What we talked about was the idea that Helo kind of senses that something's different, but doesn't really care. He doesn't *know*, but there are clues. Finally Ron Moore said, 'That's so wrong, it's right — we have to do it.'"

Nankin made the decision to shoot the entire scene from the injured Athena's segmented point of view, which meant that the final result was fragmented and indistinct. "That helped me, because with broadcast standards I couldn't actually show nudity or certain elements of sex," Nankin explains. "So it allowed me to shoot it out of focus, which actually made it more erotic. I actually had them naked — they had little pubic patches and that was it — and had them going for it."

Above: Tyrol and Boomer's brief reunion brought an even briefer happiness for the doomed couple.

Shooting a believable sex scene like this, even though it would not be seen on camera, is never an easy task for the actors. For Grace Park and Tahmoh Penikett, it helped that they had been working together for several years, and had a genuine friendship and bond. Nevertheless, Nankin still tried to make filming as private as possible. "By that time it's one big family, and the actors were game, but all non essential personnel are cleared out," the director explains. "In that set were the actors, the cameraman, the sound guy, assistant camera guy and that was it. Even I stayed out and watched it on the monitor, just to allow them as much privacy as they could get."

"Grace and I have some of the darkest, most twisted, heart wrenching scenes throughout the series," says Tahmoh Penikett. "Luckily, we've established such an excellent bond and trust in each other — we come from the same acting school, we grew up together and got our chops on this series. So oftentimes it wasn't hard for us to go to those places, even though they are very difficult scenes, because it's a safe environment, and because we have those relationships established with those excellent directors like Michael Nankin and Michael Rymer."

"It was a wonderful episode to have as my swansong," adds Nankin. "It was a very emotional experience to shoot it because I knew it was my last *Battlestar*. But to have what was essentially a musical as my goodbye was lovely." ∎

> "The first time Bear played 'All Along the Watchtower' in Joe's Bar, chills went up my spine. I was in tears." — Michael Nankin

Music has always been a significant part of *Battlestar Galactica*, even before the momentous inclusion of 'All Along the Watchtower' at the conclusion of season three. 'Someone To Watch Over Me', however, took that to an entirely different level, not least for musician Bear McCreary. His fascinating blog entries for this episode are too extensive to cover completely here, but give an enthralling insight into how the episode came together, and his involvement.

"I hold 'Someone To Watch Over Me' among the most important works of my entire career thus far," says McCreary. "My role as composer evolved far beyond merely providing underscore for the scenes. This time, I was intimately involved in every step of the episode's development."

In fact, McCreary's involvement began even before writers Bradley Thompson and David Weddle had put fingers to keyboard. Following the conclusion of episodes twelve and thirteen, the writing room had begun apportioning the last episodes of the show. Although Ron Moore was slated to write the finale, obviously all the other writers who had had such a huge input and influence on the series since its beginning had stories that they wanted to finish on — favourite characters that they wanted to bid goodbye to, perhaps, or ideas they had not yet had the chance to explore.

"We asked to do the episode that Michael Nankin was signed to direct," recalls David Weddle, "because we had developed a very intense and fulfilling collaboration with him over the course of the last two seasons."

"We had some idea it would be a Starbuck vehicle, and we had some notion that we'd get to do Boomer/Tyrol, but we definitely knew that given the choice, we'd sing our swan song with Michael," adds Bradley Thompson.

Once that had been decided, the writers began to think seriously about what they would like that final Starbuck-centric story to be. Very early on, they came up with the idea of exploring the story of Kara's relationship with her father. "By exploring her relationship with her father," says Weddle, "we could complete the story of Kara, in a way."

One of the first ideas discussed in the writers' room was that the story could flashback to Starbuck as a child, as her father taught her to play a song on the piano. It didn't take long for someone to suggest that that song be 'All Along the Watchtower'.

Opposite: The episode explored a previously unseen aspect of Kara Thrace's background — her relationship with her father.

"The second inspiration came from Ron Moore, who had the idea of Hera actually drawing the notes of 'Watchtower'," Weddle continues. "Ron said this could

enable Starbuck to remember the song at the very moment that Hera is being kidnapped. Once we had those two breakthroughs, the story fell into place very rapidly."

As discussions continued, the flashbacks all but disappeared, replaced by the idea that Kara meets her musician father — without recognising him — in Joe's Bar aboard the *Galactica*. Once they had hit on the idea of 'Slick' and Kara interacting over the composition of a song, the writers knew it was already time to involve Bear McCreary. They didn't only want McCreary's input into the music — they wanted his advice about Slick's character. Moore had pointed out that he needed to have his own arc — conflicts, triumphs, frustrations — if he was not to seem obviously a phantom figure. "Ron Moore did not like the voice of the piano player in the early drafts," recalls Weddle. "He felt the character came off like a stock bartender/wise-man from a 100 other movies."

The writers recorded several conversations with McCreary wherein they talked about a variety of topics surrounding music, music genres, composition and more. At the time, McCreary was busy producing a series of *Battlestar Galactica* music concerts in Los Angeles, as well as scoring the music for 'Revelations'. The pressures of the two combined were immense, and caused McCreary to temporarily suffer the musician's version of 'writer's block'. In the midst of this, Weddle called up to ask McCreary more about the life of a musician, and, as serendipity would have it, wanted to know specifically about how a musician copes when a composition is being troublesome. "I vented all my creative frustration in the most vulnerable conversation I've ever had with a producer who held my job in his hands," reveals McCreary. "We spoke not only of dealing with writer's block and creative frustration, but of the intense pressure that I have always felt to create something artistically worthwhile."

These conversations with McCreary allowed the writers to really understand the creative musical mind, and develop a believable character in Slick. Some of those conversations couldn't have influenced the script more directly. "There's a scene where Slick confesses his writer's block and tells Kara that he's been 'at it for four days now. It's Hell.'" McCreary says. "Those were my exact words when David called me."

With the script done, McCreary was also invited to the set for filming. The production had found an excellent actor to play Slick (Roark Critchlow) who was also a sight-reading pianist. He also rehearsed the duet with Katee Sackhoff. Sackhoff revealed that she had been made to learn piano as a child, and used the memories of that childhood discontent to tap into Starbuck's reaction to and relationship with the pianist in Joe's Bar. "I hated it," she says, of those piano lessons. "There are teeth marks on my father's old baby grand from me biting the piano when I was bored!"

McCreary's presence on set for filming meant that he was not only able to have a cameo as a fully kitted-out extra, but that he could play the music live on set once Critchlow and Sackhoff had wrapped their scenes.

"When Kara began to play 'Watchtower', the script called for them to recognise the song and walk over to her," McCreary explains. "For these close ups, the piano

wasn't on camera, so Michael asked me to play my arrangement of 'Watchtower' to help inspire their reactions."

For director Michael Nankin, being able to have that music live on set added something that he could never have achieved without McCreary's input. "It was thrilling to hear," he says. "I love working with music on the set — especially the music that's going to end up in the final version of the picture. The first time Bear played 'All Along the Watchtower' in Joe's Bar, chills went up my spine. I was in tears."

In fact, the music of 'Someone To Watch Over Me' affected McCreary so deeply that he continued to think about it long after the conclusion of *Battlestar Galactica*. "Kara's dad is composing all through the episode," says Nankin. "He's struggling with it, and you hear snatches and bits and pieces. Bear McCreary wasn't satisfied with that, so he sat down and wrote the entire sonata!"

'Slick's Sonata', as it was called (its actual name is Dreilide Thrace Sonata No.1), received its first public performance in a live show produced specifically to showcase McCreary's *Battlestar Galactica* score. "Bear and the *Battlestar Galactica* orchestra did a live performance in downtown Los Angeles, and it was the world premiere of Slick's Sonata," says Nankin, who was one of the 2,500-strong audience at California Plaza in the opening concert of the Grand Performances Summer Music Festival on 13 June 2009. "It was magnificent." ∎

Above: The theme of 'All Along the Watchtower' held significance not only for Starbuck, but also for the Cylon residents aboard *Galactica*.

[ISLANDED IN A STREAM OF STARS]

WRITTEN BY: Michael Taylor
DIRECTED BY: Edward
James Olmos

GUEST CAST: Kate Vernon (Ellen Tigh), Donnelly Rhodes (Dr. Cottle), Dean Stockwell (John Cavil), Bodie Olmos (Lieutenant Brenden 'Hotdog' Costanza), David Patrick Green (Xeno Fenner), Kerry Norton (Medic Layne Ishay), Iliana Gomez-Martinez (Hera Agathon), Laura Gilchrist (Paulla Schaffer), Leela Savasta (Tracey Anne), Darcy Laurie (Dealino), Susan Hogan (Captain Doyle Franks), William Samples (Captain Jules Tarney), Curtis Caravaggio (Marine Nathanson)

"I've had it up to here with destiny, prophecy, with God or the Gods.
Look where it's left us. The ass end of nowhere." — William Adama

Galactica continues to fall apart — a hull breach kills more than sixty human and Cylon workers. In the wake of Hera's kidnapping, Ellen reveals she would have been taken to a construct called 'The Colony' for experimentation. Adama sends a Heavy Raider on a recon mission, but is unwilling to send the whole fleet, and refuses Helo a Raptor for his own search. The Colony has already moved from Ellen's coordinates.

On the stolen Raptor, Boomer is becoming tired of Hera's terrified crying, but eventually the two bond, and when they arrive at the Colony, Boomer finds herself reluctant to give the child up to Cavil.

Meanwhile, Starbuck, still desperate to find out what she is, explains what she found on Earth to Baltar and asks him to run some tests. He matches the blood on her dogtags — it belongs to Kara Thrace. He announces this at the funeral for those killed in the hull breach, calling her an angel. She visits Anders, who is still comatose and has been placed in a hybrid tank. Kara intends to shoot him, but he grabs her hand and begins to speak like a hybrid. The polymer used on *Galactica* has allowed Anders to fuse with the ship, meaning he is connected to her FTL drive.

Adama realises that it's the end of the line for his beloved ship, and tells Tigh that they will abandon the *Galactica*.

Michael Angeli, interviewed along with this episode's writer Michael Taylor, by Maureen Ryan at her *Chicago Tribune* blog, calls 'Islanded in a Stream of Stars' the "threshold". It's an excellent description. For weeks, *Galactica* has been — literally as well as physically — teetering on the brink of an abyss, as the ship continues to fall apart and Adama realises that he has nowhere safe to take the surviving human fleet. It was also the final standard-length episode before the epic finale to an already epic series.

Opposite: Tigh is as attached to *Galactica* as Admiral Adama is, and does not want to abandon ship.

Given all of those factors, not to mention Adama's momentous decision that *Galactica* would have to be abandoned, it seems fitting that the episode was helmed by Edward James Olmos.

"I thought it was incredible," the actor says of the script. "It was an honour [to direct]. It was a brilliant piece of work, and I thought that we went on to do a strong job. It started off with a really intense sequence before the show starts, a prologue at the beginning that was very, very complex in its storytelling and the way that we had to shoot it."

Olmos is here referring to the hull-breach scenes, which begin with a human and a Six almost coming to blows, and in the next moment the Six is sacrificing her life to save the human. "At one point the big disaster with the space-flushed Six occurred in the middle of the story," Angeli reveals. "Mike recognised that he needed to start the story hot and moved it, with great success, to the teaser."

Another particularly intense scene occurs between Helo and Athena, both distraught following the kidnapping of Hera and Helo's inadvertent infidelity with Boomer. It's a scene that particularly sticks in Olmos's mind, and is one of his favourites of the episode. "I was so proud of both Tahmoh and Grace," he recalls. "These two actors were probably, at the beginning of the series, the youngest and the newest to the medium of all the kids that were working on the show. They had had experience, but they hadn't had very much, so they were learning as we were doing it. But, by the time we got to these performances at the end, it was magnificent to watch them work, because they had done an extraordinary job of learning the craft during that time. I was watching in amazement — as everybody else was — as to what was going on in front of the camera. Nothing was said to them; nothing was needed to be said to them. They were probably the most prepared they had ever been, and it shows. You see the moments between Helo and Athena when they are in their cabin, and they're trying desperately hard to hang on to their sanity. And she just looks at him — she didn't say anything, she didn't *have* to. Those moments were just breathtaking, and really beautifully performed."

However modest Olmos may be in insisting that little direction was required for the scene, writer Michael Taylor believes that Olmos's skill as a director lays in the rapport he builds with his cast, and in his deep understanding of human emotion. "He's able to probe beneath the surface of any given scene and tap into the raw welter of emotions undergirding it," says Taylor. "It's like he's constantly pushing to find some deeper inchoate, something that a sieve of words alone can't trap."

SURVEILLANCE: ADDITIONAL

'Islanded in a Stream of Stars' also features some of the last scenes between Starbuck and the incapacitated Anders. For actor Michael Trucco, this meant spending rather a lot of time partly submerged in a tank of fluid. "It was very odd," he says of the experience. "It's fun for the first twenty minutes, but then days of it, for hours at a time… it became a little tedious at times! It was difficult because you're in that awkward position in that water and you're wearing next to nothing — just this little skin-coloured Speedo! So there's a certain amount of humiliation that went along with getting in and out of the tub every time, and I was in a bald cap that was four-and-a-half hours of make-up to put on every morning. So there was a certain discomfort to it at the time. But it's nothing now. At the time you're like, 'God how many more days of this do I have to do?' But once I saw the finished product and realised that it was a pretty important part of the story — Anders being able to drive the fleet into the sun, ultimately — it made it all worth it, definitely."

Olmos also loved the scene between Roslin and Adama in which Laura movingly convinces the Admiral that it's time to leave *Galactica*. "That's when Mary gives one of the great performances of her character," the actor states. "She sits there and tells me that she never felt like she had a home until she got onboard the ship and lived with me there for the few months that they were together, and it was really sad that I didn't realise that there was a possibility that I would lose both of them at the same time if I didn't get us off the ship. It was a very, very powerful moment."

Of course, in shooting that scene, Olmos couldn't simply absorb himself in the playing of it — it was down to him to stage and shoot it, too. Like many of the cast, McDonnell and Olmos had been working together for so long by the time this scene came along that extensive discussion about how the two characters would interact here was unnecessary. But Olmos still had to find a way to shoot the emotion and acceptance of the scene. "I went in for the close-ups first, so that the performances were strikingly powerful and passionate from the beginning," he explains. "Then we just worked them out — over the shoulders first, and I gave it to her and then she gave it back to me, and then we went for the wide shots. Those are much easier. But it was amazing — I've got to say that the last four hours of this programme, starting with the one that I directed, all the way to the end — the performances between Laura and Adama are some of the most rewarding performances that I've given."

Though Olmos was thrilled with what was shot for the episode, his director's cut ran twenty-six minutes long, and as a result had to be severely cut. Thanks to DVD technology, however, viewers are able to view the extended director's cut as part of the season four box set, something the actor-director is eminently glad about. "The DVD long version of that is really so different," he says. "It's remarkable. It's not only performance different, it is night and day different, because there are scenes that are not in the television version and there are also some scenes that are just cut to shreds. [There were] performances between Helo and Kara, scenes between the Chief and Athena, scenes with Boomer and the baby that were [all] very, very powerful and important that you never saw. It's really sad."

Of course, one of the most memorable scenes of the episode is performed by Edward James Olmos himself. A devastated Admiral Adama, finally realising that *Galactica* is perishing, surrenders to a period of abject grief. "That's not just Adama mud-wrestling in the paint with his sense of loss," says Angeli, who was on set for the filming of that scene. "That's Eddie realising that all of the excitement, the thrill, the rain, the few gorgeous days of Vancouver sun, the hard work, the good battles, the friendships, the sublime routines, the character he inhabited for almost six years were coming to an end. For that scene Eddie just kept the camera rolling — no takes — until he was spent." ■

SURVEILLANCE: ADDITIONAL

Edward James Olmos was not the intended director of this episode. "I wasn't scheduled to direct that piece," the actor reveals. "Frank Darabont was scheduled to direct it, and Frank has done a lot of great work in film. So I wasn't really thinking about it — and then all of a sudden, Frank couldn't make it. And so about six days before we were about to shoot, they handed me the script and asked me if I would direct it."

[DAYBREAK]

WRITTEN BY: Ron Moore
DIRECTED BY: Michael Rymer

GUEST CAST: Kate Vernon (Ellen Tigh), Rick Worthy (Simon), Donnelly Rhodes (Dr. Cottle), Mark Sheppard (Romo Lampkin), Matthew Bennett (Aaron Doral), Kerry Norton (Medic Layne Ishay), Dean Stockwell (John Cavil), Bodie Olmos (Lieutenant Brenden 'Hotdog' Costanza), Leah Cairns (Lieutenant Margaret 'Racetrack' Edmonson), Colin Lawrence (Lieutenant Hamish 'Skulls' McCall), Brad Dryborough (Lieutenant Louis Hoshi), Jennifer Halley (Ensign Diana 'Hardball' Seelix), Laura Gilchrist (Paulla Schaffer), Colin Corrigan (Marine Allan Nowart), Leela Savasta (Tracey Anne), Darcy Laurie (Dealino), Finn R. Devitt (Nicky Tyrol), Iliana Gomez-Martinez (Hera Agathon), Tobias Mehler (Zak Adama), Antony Hollan (Julius Baltar), Simone Bailly (Shona), Elan Ross Gibson (Nurse Barbara), France Perras (Sandra Roslin), Sarah Deakins (Cheryl Roslin), Tiffany Burns (Reporter Carolyn), Kevin McNulty (Frank Porthos), Stefanie Samuels (Police Officer), Richard Jollymore (Marine #1), Anthony St. John (Marine #2), Dan Payne (Sean Ellison), Holly Eglinton (Stripper)

"Galactica has seen a lot of history, gone through a lot of battles. This will be her last. She will not fail us if we do not fail her. If we succeed in our mission, *Galactica* will bring us home. If we don't... It doesn't matter anyway." — William Adama

---

Through a series of flashbacks, we see the crew of *Galactica* as they were before the Cylon attack on the Colonies. Lee Adama meets Kara Thrace for the first time; Baltar takes Caprica Six to his home, where she meets his abusive father. Roslin throws a baby shower for her pregnant sister, only to discover later that both her sisters and father have been killed in a car accident. Three months later, she joins Mayor Adar's campaign. Anders gives a post-game interview.

In the present, the stripping of *Galactica* has begun. Everything useful is to be salvaged, and military control is to be transferred to the Basestar. Baltar asks Lee to give his cult a place on the Quorum, but he is refused. As he walks past the wall of remembrance, Adama spots a picture of Hera. He takes it down, making a decision. After giving amnesty to Tyrol, who has been imprisoned for helping Boomer escape, he issues a statement. There will be a mission to retrieve Hera. It will be dangerous, and not everyone will survive. Adama calls for volunteers. The final five volunteer, as does a very weak Roslin.

A Raptor is sent to find the Colony, and locates it at the edge of a black hole. Despite the risks, Adama orders the attack to begin. *Galactica* will jump in with its crew of volunteers and ram the Colony, while Anders connects to the Colony's hybrid, and persuades it to stop firing. Two Raptor teams will enter the Colony via the hole made by *Galactica*'s assault and retrieve Hera.

The plan works, although it takes more time than anticipated for Anders to power down the Colony, and the ship takes a brutal pounding. The Cylons attack *Galactica*, boarding the ship as the volunteers, including Caprica Six and Baltar, desperately fight to hold them off. The Raptor holding Racetrack is hit, killing its occupants instantly.

In the Colony, the two assault teams, lead by Starbuck and Apollo and aided by the now-sentient rebel Centurions, struggle to locate Hera. Boomer, trying to atone for her earlier actions, frees the child and brings her to Athena and Helo, also part of the rescue team. Athena shoots Boomer dead, and the teams return to *Galactica*, where the fight is still continuing.

Cavil, discovering Hera has gone, takes a Centurion escort and heads for *Galactica*. Helo is shot and badly wounded. As Athena tries to stop him bleeding out, a terrified Hera runs away. Athena and Roslin follow her, and, as they see Six pick her up, realise this is the realisation of their shared dream. They follow Baltar, Six and Hera, finding themselves in CIC — the dreamed of 'Opera House'.

Above: Karl 'Helo' Agathon joins the fight to save his daughter.

Cavil, reaching CIC, takes Hera at gunpoint and threatens to kill her. Tigh, speaking for the final five, promises to give him the secrets of resurrection if the conflict ends here. Cavil agrees, and calls off the Cylon assault on *Galactica*. The five connect to the Colony hybrid via Anders — they all have part of the secret and all have to pass it on simultaneously. As they are doing so, Tyrol has access to Tory's memories and sees what she did to Cally. Enraged, he breaks the contact and snaps her neck. Cavil, thinking they've been caught in a trap, knowing his fellow 'skinjobs' are dead, shoots himself. The battle begins again, and *Galactica* cannot take the strain, buckling as the Cylons renew their assault. Racetrack's Raptor is hit by a meteorite, the shock of which forces the dead Lieutenant's hand into launching its nukes at the Colony.

The Colony, severely damaged, begins to fall into the black hole, taking *Galactica* with it. Adama tells Starbuck to jump, anywhere, it doesn't matter where. Struck by a moment of inspiration, Kara keys in the numbers she assigned to the notes drawn by Hera. *Galactica* survives the jump, but only just, breaking her back under the strain.

Where they are is where they're going to stay — but on the horizon is a blue-green planet. Discovering that its primitive inhabitants share the Colonials' DNA, the survivors settle there, abandoning the bulk of their technology and sending their fleet of ships into the sun with Anders at *Galactica*'s helm. Adama takes the dying Roslin to find a place they can build their wished-for cabin. Laura dies before Adama can set down, and he buries her on a ridge above a lush plain. Starbuck, having accomplished her purpose, says goodbye to Lee and vanishes. The rest of the population spreads out to different parts of the planet. 150,000 years later, Head Baltar and Head Six wander through the streets of a crowded New York City, wondering if the cycle is about to repeat itself...

And so to the end. There was never any question that Ron Moore would write the ending to *Battlestar Galactica*'s long journey through space. But how to accomplish that? How is it possible to satisfactorily end a saga five years in the making; a saga that in its five years on air had generated such intense interest, debate and passion among both its creators and its viewers? Not an easy task, for sure, and one that required a somewhat different approach in the writers' room.

GALACTICA'S DEMISE

The ship the Battlestar *Galactica* was absolutely integral to the series. Besides lending her name to the show, she was where most of the action of the series had taken place — and so choosing the right away for her to make her exit was important.

"Once we had decided that *Galactica* was going to get to Earth in the distant past, the question was, 'Well, what are we going to do with the ship?'" says Ron Moore. "We played around with that quite a bit in the fourth season."

The writers discussed various options before making the decision to send *Galactica* and the rest of the fleet into the sun. "At one point we talked about maybe burying the ship, and maybe in a flash forward to contemporary times, there were these mounds of unknown origin in Central America," recalls Moore. "That was something Bradley Thompson was talking about. We were going to have somebody digging into one of these mounds and discovering metal — and there would be the side of the ship. We also had a version where Adama decided to burn the *Galactica*, like Cortez burning his ships when he got to the New World."

Finally, though, Moore realised that the Colonials wouldn't just get rid of *Galactica*. They would abandon all their ships, *all* their technology. "The whole show is predicated on the idea of technology that had turned against them, and that all of this has happened before and all of it would happen again," Moore points out. "It seemed like when they got to Earth, somebody should say, 'Here's this pastoral world, which doesn't have this technology, and are we really going to bring it all with us all over again?' Especially since they just did this back on New Caprica, and it ended in disaster. There was just something poetic about it — leave it behind. Don't take your baggage with you — let's have a fresh start."

"I wanted to find it on the page," explains Moore, "I didn't want to figure it all out until I was doing it. So it was broken a little differently. We did spend time in the writers' room talking about it, and we did break the general outline of what was going to happen and we broke out what the flashbacks were about, but I didn't write a formal outline for it. I just sat down and wrote the script."

"It was sort of like '33'," adds David Eick, "in that there was a lot of discussion about it in a very macro sense. There were storylines that had been building that needed to be resolved, so to that extent, there was a plan. It's not as though Ron went into it with no idea what he was going to write after 'Fade In'. But at the same time, it was much less painstakingly broken and figured out as a plot or as a character piece than any other episode that I can remember, going all the way back to the first and the final episodes of the first season."

"I just wanted a looser break," Moore says, simply. "Guideposts, directions and a general sort of schematic of what I was trying to accomplish. I really liked just sitting down and figuring out what the cut would be — going from this scene to the next scene, to the next scene and the next scene. I wrote it without act breaks, almost like a movie, just straight through. I just wanted it to flow, and it did. And that's just how it worked."

The question of how the fleet's journey would resolve itself has been a matter of debate amongst fans since the airing of the Miniseries. Eick reveals, however, that no matter what else changed during the show's run, Moore had always kept two desires for the conclusion constant. So, when he went into writing the finale, those were the first two points on the show's "schematic". "There was a big idea that everyone knew and that Ron and I had discussed a long time ago that we knew we had to hit, which was how it was going to end," says Eick. "The arrival at a planet that they will now christen Earth, even though it's not the real Earth. And we are in a prehistoric time, the revelation being that the characters of *Battlestar* are our ancestors, not our descendants. So that was the big idea that we always wanted to do."

Above: Baltar and Six, as they will be remembered.

Perhaps more surprising is the other element that had emerged early on and stayed — the coda scene, featuring Head Six and Head Baltar on the streets of present-day New York. "I think Ron and I first had that conversation at the end of season one, or somewhere in season two," Eick recalls. "It was [there] to reinforce the ironic punch line, that they are not our descendants, they are our ancestors, and their forms are still here. It was just such a crisp way of selling that idea. There were certain details that came later, like looking at contemporary robots in store windows, and certainly the dialogue of the scene wasn't there until Ron wrote it. But conceptually, it's one of the things that most closely matches in execution what the idea was from the beginning, than anything else in the entire run of the series."

Not all of the production staff liked the idea of bringing *Galactica* to an Earth so unambiguously linked to reality. "I know Ron was determined to bring the world of *Battlestar Galactica* to our world, and I was always a little nervous [of that]," confesses director Michael Rymer. "I thought that, because the show was so allegorical, they were parallel tracks that should never meet. To some extent I still feel that, but I think we got away with it. We brought these two worlds together and because people are so emotionally invested in the show, they are prepared to suspend disbelief that little bit further and longer than they ever had to before."

Something that everyone did love in Moore's script was his flashback concept. Instead of remaining solely in the fraught, terrifying present, the story went back to

EDWARD JAMES OLMOS

"I was very, very happy with everything that occurred at the end. I had no qualms about it — I just wanted more! There was just a desire to continue to work, really, and not to stop — we just wanted to keep going and tell more of the story. [But] I think it was a good idea to end it where they did. I think it left everybody with a strong sense of love for the whole project. It worked really well."

pre-attack Caprica, to give the audience a glimpse of what each character had been like before their individual tragedies began.

"The flashbacks *are* the story," states Eick, emphatically, about why those scenes are there. "The flashbacks are really the A story of the finale, in that they finish a picture — a painting — that you've seen all but the first pieces of, one you can't ever really entirely understand or appreciate [without them]. I feel they were more than just, 'Here's what the characters were doing before the attack,' — it's, 'Here's what the characters *were*.' And in knowing who they were, you have a completely different understanding of what it means to see who they are now, who they have become."

"It was important realise that who they were at the beginning really does tell you why they ended up as they were at the very end," adds Moore. "So it was really about beginnings and endings and having a continuum between the two."

As was to be expected, particularly with a *Battlestar Galactica* script, Moore's first draft (which was in fact very close to what ended up being the final, shooting draft) came in very over long. And, as was also expected, the first thing the network suggested cutting were the flashbacks. Determined that they should stay in, Moore and Eick went to bat for the concept, and succeeded in keeping them as an integral part of the finale script — although the battle to keep them in the show was not yet over.

Having written how the characters began all those years before, and having spent so long bringing them to life in the intervening time, Moore now had to write their ends. For some of them — Laura Roslin, for example — their conclusions were obvious, inevitable. For others, what they had become through the course of the series meant their endings were far more ephemeral. But for all of them, this was the *end* — and surely it must have been a difficult thing for their creator to write.

"It was and it wasn't," says Moore. "I didn't connect with it emotionally on the page as much — I didn't take time to feel Laura's death as I was writing it [for example]. It was a lot of pressure — internal pressure to make it good, and feeling like I was not going to make it good and it was going to suck and people were going to hate it, and time was running out, and I was getting calls for other demands on my time from editing to visual effects and this and that. There was a lot of chaos going on at the same time. So during the writing process, I really didn't have a sense of closure to any of it — it was all just trying to get it done."

As previously mentioned, Moore's first draft of 'Daybreak' ended up being almost completely identical to the version that was shot. Before it actually reached that stage, however, Moore reveals that he made one significant change. "Initially, we talked about Laura and Adama just getting into the Raptor and flying off into the stars never to be seen again," he says. "Word came back from Mary [McDonnell] that she had always counted on having a death scene at the end of the show. And I had always promised her that she would have a death scene at the end, and I thought, 'You know what, she's right. I'm going to play it on camera. She'll get to Earth and we'll just play it out.'"

MARY McDONNELL

"That was such a wonderful thing for a writer to do for an actress. [Ron Moore] didn't realise he was doing me such a favour, but he allowed me as an actress in the last episode to also play young and vital again. So that the audience and the fans and the people who know her, their last image of her isn't just of a dying woman. They get to remember — and even be introduced — to a woman they never knew."

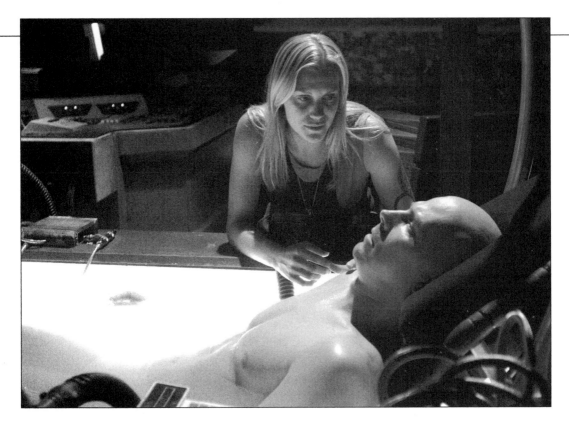

Director Michael Rymer also had a note for Moore, in which he suggested that it was rather lucky — and possibly a little unbelievable — that most of the characters survived to the end. Rymer actually discussed the possibility of further characters dying with Tahmoh Penikett, since the most likely candidates for a tragic end were Helo and Athena. "I said to Tahmoh, 'How do you feel about that?' And he said, 'Well, I hear what you're saying, but I would counter that by saying that it's sort of obvious. If you kill me, it feels predictable.' I thought that was a very good argument. And now, looking at the end, the resonance of Laura's death is so profound and so organic to the show, you didn't need to have a very high body count to really feel like you'd pulled it off in a satisfying, complete way — and it might have taken away from that. As it turned out, in the way it was shot we had our cake and got to eat it, too, because when Sharon runs off to get Hera and leaves Helo bleeding to death, we don't see him for the longest time. It's assumed that he's dead. So his appearance at the end became a story point. It became a beat, a twist, which added to the end."

With the shooting script ready to go, Michael Rymer stepped in to prepare for filming.

Above: Kara Thrace bids a sad goodbye to her husband, Samuel Anders.

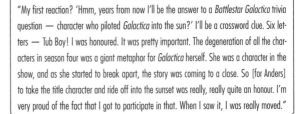

MICHAEL TRUCCO

"My first reaction? 'Hmm, years from now I'll be the answer to a *Battlestar Galactica* trivia question — character who piloted *Galactica* into the sun?' I'll be a crossword clue. Six letters — Tub Boy! I was honoured. It was pretty important. The degeneration of all the characters in season four was a giant metaphor for *Galactica* herself. She was a character in the show, and as she started to break apart, the story was coming to a close. So [for Anders] to take the title character and ride off into the sunset was really, really quite an honour. I'm very proud of the fact that I got to participate in that. When I saw it, I was really moved."

Rymer, a cornerstone of the *Battlestar Galactica* production team, had directed the Miniseries and many of the show's most momentous episodes. And, looking at the story of the finale, he knew immediately what was likely to cause the most problems in post production.

"When we got 'Daybreak', we were just enraptured with the script," Rymer recalls. "And I think the cast and I really understood that what was vulnerable was the flashbacks. We knew that the big battle and the resolution, and the tying up of all the emotional threads of the series was going to take priority, but we all loved the flashbacks. So we all really focused on trying to find ways of making them as compelling as the main story, just as a way to make sure they got into the final cut."

"They did surprise me, and it took me a minute to navigate so that I understood," confesses Mary McDonnell. "But in terms of ending a saga, I think the flashbacks were amazing in that they just slowed us down. We were hurtling, literally, towards the end, and they kept slowing us down to reminisce about who these people were. They're just *people*. Before all this, they were people who had lives that were limited, and human, and funny, and terrible. And then the next day they were the only surviving people of millions and millions. A day earlier, a day before the Miniseries occurred, they were just people. But then immediately we leave the flashbacks and come to who they are now — and they're the future of mankind. That's crazy, right?" the actress laughs. "That's amazing. That's what I personally loved about the flashbacks. That's what they did for me."

One of Rymer's personal favourites from the flashback sequences was the story of Baltar, his father, and Caprica Six — even though both he and James Callis at first had trouble working through the content. "The whole arc between James and Tricia in those flashbacks was so interesting and strong. James and I were a little bit nervous because there was so much revisionism going on. We were reading this script going, 'Okay, fine — so he gave her the secrets that betrayed humanity because she got to him emotionally, because she did such a good thing for his father, and they had a deep connection. But in the Mini, it's pretty clear that what's going on is mainly lascivious. It's about sex for secrets,'" the director points out. "But we really liked it anyway, so we said, 'Okay, we're going to go for it and pull it off and really go for a deep connection between Baltar and Six in a way that we never expected.' I think that pays off in the very final scene when they're on the planet and he breaks down. You see that he's finally accepting his father in a way he never could when he was alive. But there was that final, final scene between Baltar and Six where they meet in the Caprica square, and he says, 'What men will do for love,' and she says, 'Love, Gaius?' and they smile at each other. It becomes more ironic, less purely romantic, and it sort of brings it back full circle."

Rymer also credits James Callis's talents in making Baltar's final chronological scene so compelling. "On Earth, where he breaks down and says, 'I know how to farm' — that was improvised; it wasn't scripted that he would break down and be emotional,

Above: For every fan who had wondered where Lee and Kara's attraction had started, this flashback had the answer: at first sight.

James found that in the scene when we were shooting it. And it starts with Ron's brilliant script, but the brilliance of these actors filling in around the edges and creating the emotional coherence of it all just took it to another level."

Tricia Helfer also appreciated the added depth that the flashbacks gave to Caprica Six. As she points out, the audience had only ever seen the end of Baltar and Six's relationship, and never the beginning. "I think it showed more of her emotional capability, that she really did *feel* these things," the actress says. "She finds Baltar's father a home where he can be a much happier man, and that in itself was going to make Baltar happier, too. But I don't necessarily think that she did that for Baltar, she did it because she felt that was right. I think it just shows a deeper level of connection between these two characters, and why it was good that they end up together."

The flashbacks also gave the actors an opportunity to show the audience the point at which they had become the people we had followed for five years. For Katee Sackhoff, that meant being able to show where Starbuck's inner darkness came from, a darkness that had dogged her since before the Cylon attack. "Katee said to me, 'Starbuck was always brash, but the darkness in Starbuck that we started seeing as early as the Miniseries did not exist until she caused the death of her fiancé,'" Rymer recalls. "And so if you look at what Katee's doing, she's a lot sweeter and a more innocent version of Starbuck, even though she can still drink anyone under the table."

To enhance the pace of the flashbacks, Rymer decided to shoot those scenes differently, in a choppier, faster style. "There's a lot of energy in them. The camera never settles, it's always wandering and moving around and readjusting," he points out.

JAMIE BAMBER

"What I love about the whole ending is you get to go back and see the characters as they are at the beginning of the Miniseries, or even before that. You get to see what they were like before they were messed up, and that journey, for Lee, starts with Starbuck."

"I didn't want the flashbacks to just lie there. The show already has a lot of visual energy so I had to keep saying to the camera operators, 'Remember, this is a flashback, make it even crazier!' It worked really well because when you get to the last hour, when we're on Earth, there's virtually no hand-held — most of it is on steadicam or dollies."

Aside from the complexity of the flashbacks, Rymer had a massive story to tell that included a daring rescue and a huge, prolonged battle sequence that took place on several levels. Considering the epic nature of the basic story of *Battlestar Galactica* — the survival of the human race — it's curious that the climax is precipitated by the decision to rescue one child.

"There was something about the smallness of it," says Moore, of why he chose that catalyst. "The one life, the one little girl. Even though Adama had the responsibility for all these thousands of lives and the future of humanity, he could still be moved and touched by the plight of one, and there would still be a part of him that would feel that he had left her behind and he couldn't live with that. He didn't want that on his conscience and he felt a strong pull to go back for her."

The emotional aspects of the more action-oriented sequences in 'Daybreak' were welcomed by Rymer, who found them a useful tool in tempering the hectic pace of the finale. "There was a lot of action, and it was complicated," he says, "but the thing I'm most proud of is that in pretty much every action scene, there's still something really subtle and interesting going on between the characters."

Two examples given by Rymer come within the same sequence — as Baltar and Six hunker down and wait for Cavil's forces to board *Galactica*. "There are all these lovely little moments between them as they are preparing for battle. And then Lee comes through after Lee and Baltar have had so much conflict. Baltar's firing in a panic and then apologises to Lee, and Lee goes, 'No, no — You did *good*, doc'. It's a very brief moment, but it completes a story arc that we had going in a very organic, emotional way, and yet we're in the heat of battle. Battle scenes are only meaningful to me if there's some sort of emotional resonance — if we give a shit. It's not about the pyrotechnics; it's about the people and what's at stake. I have strange favourites, but that's certainly one of my favourite scenes in 'Daybreak'."

Rymer also says that in terms of directing, 'Daybreak' proved challenging not only because of the amount of story he had to tell, but the way in which Moore had written it. *Galactica* episodes generally run long and need to be cut in post, so experienced directors like Rymer have learned to frame each scene so that it can fit almost anywhere in an edit, rather than just the place it was written to fit. With 'Daybreak'

TAHMOH PENIKETT

I think it was an excellent finale, I really do. I think you'd be hard pressed to find any show that could have an ending as epic and conclusive as that and, at the same time, leaving so many questions. Which I think is what a good series like this should be like. It's up to interpretation, there have to be questions — there can't be conclusions to *all* the storylines. You want to leave it up to the audience's imagination somewhat, because we'd been through so much and our fans have been through so much. You couldn't get that feel with a feature. There are a lot of different opinions out there, but there's always going to be; that's how we are. But for the most part, most of the fans I've spoken to loved it."

Above: Caprica Six and Gaius Baltar, reunited at last.

the deliberate style in which it was written gave the director an added challenge.

"I had my hands full just getting these massive stories told in an efficient way," says Rymer, "and 'Daybreak' was full of these very quick little expositional pieces that all joined up together into one conversation. That's something Ron had never done before, and it certainly required a very focused attention to rhythm and pacing. I tend to shoot lots of introductions and transitions in and out, knowing that these pieces might get rearranged. But in 'Daybreak', that was particularly hard — and I loved the scripts of 'Daybreak' so much I particularly wanted to keep a brisk rhythm going so there was room to fit it all in."

Despite the cuts that were made before the episode shot, and the efforts that Rymer made to keep the pace up during shooting, the editor's initial assembly for 'Daybreak' came in at over four hours long. Moore's first thought was to try to get the network to let *Battlestar Galactica* have another hour of screen time.

"When I went into the editing room Ron said, 'Let me know if you think it's four hours, because that's a battle I'll have to fight.' After I looked at it I called him and said, 'I don't think this is four hours. It's too slow, it's too fat — we can get this down to three.'

As Rymer suspected, the network's first suggestion was to slash the flashback scenes. "Sure enough, the network said 'We love the show, but these flashbacks are slow and they're tangential. Can we get rid of them? Can we cut them back?' And we did trim some of them, but not out of proportion with anything else."

"There were more flashbacks between Tyrol and Boomer and Helo," Moore

GRACE PARK

"I feel really satisfied with how things ended up. I was always curious as to what was going to happen to Boomer and Athena, and I thought this was a beautiful way of doing it — they collided, [with] the death of one of them, which I didn't expect. I was really satisfied with the way everything ended — and on top of that, how not everybody lived. But not everybody died, and not everyone died in the same manner. It was beautiful."

Above: Admiral William Adama's emotional call for volunteers to rescue Hera Agathon.

explains of the cut flashbacks, "showing where their relationship began, in lighter moments, and seeing when their first kiss was. Cally finding out, Helo being torn for his feelings for Boomer, and realising that she's in love with another man — that was probably the biggest story. The rest were dropped scenes here and there that were painful to lose in the editing process, but you could do without, and, again, most of those were restored for the DVD version."

'Daybreak' changed considerably during the editing process as the director and producers tried to work out the best way to assemble the story in the screen time they had. "This is one of those shows that was so much fun to edit. There was so much material, there were so many permutations of what one could do," Rymer explains. "In the original draft of 'Daybreak', the flashbacks were all out of order. That whole restructure actually happened after my cut. I did a cut where I put them all in chronological order, so that at least you could get some sense of flow. But people were still confused, so Ron put half the flashbacks at the front of the episode and made them not flashbacks — made them a sort of 'before the attack' sequence — which I think was the smart thing to do. Because what he had written was so beautiful and poetic, but in a narrative was hard to follow."

During filming, Rymer had deliberately paced what he calls "the red line" scene — in which Adama asks for mission volunteers — so that he could play it long. "I didn't want to waste a lot of screen time getting out a lot of exposition because I wanted to make sure there was plenty of time to build the red line scene. That's a very expanded scene time-wise," he explains, "[and] I just wanted to make sure that was protected, and we weren't suddenly going to have to short-hand that."

Unfortunately, in the final edit, the scene did have to be truncated to save time elsewhere. "Ron had to take some time out of that from the director's cut," says Rymer. "It did diminish the emotional impact of Laura showing up. But that's just a necessity of what happens in television."

There was also discussion about how the episode would be split for screening. As it had originally been written as one movie-style script, Moore had initially hoped that 'Daybreak' could be broadcast as a three-hour special. Unfortunately, the network could only accommodate a two-hour special broadcast, which meant that the first part of 'Daybreak' needed to be cut as a standard-length episode. "I was arguing for two one-and-a-half hours as a two-parter," says Rymer, "which made the mid-point

Above: 'Head' Baltar and 'Head' Six — the apparently eternal survivors of *Battlestar Galactica*'s journey.

pretty much exactly where Adama says 'Jump' and they start going into battle. I think the way the episodes were divided for the broadcast was actually quite damaging, because showing that first hour, which was quite flashback-heavy with not a hell of a lot happening, was sort of frustrating."

Despite the hard work and inevitable frustrations that went along with concluding *Battlestar Galactica*'s epic run, the cast and crew were more than happy with how the finale turned out. Though fan reactions were somewhat divided, it's probably fair to say that however the series had concluded its run, someone would always have been unhappy somewhere. Ending a story of such magnitude in a way that satisfies everyone was surely impossible — but the *Battlestar Galactica* producers, cast and crew created an exceptional three-hour end to an extraordinary five-year run.

"The ending of the series turned out to be so pastoral and beautiful and moving, and slow; all the things that the show hadn't been," says Michael Rymer. "And that was certainly our experience finishing the show. I find this about anything I shoot — what happens in front of the camera and what happens behind the camera tend to impact each other. We had a great script, we knew that we had the potential to do our best work, and we all knew this was the last time we would all be together in this particular way. So we were very much in the moment, appreciating and enjoying each other and the experience of finishing the show. There were a lot of goodbyes and lot of tears and a lot of hugs and a lot of laughs. And I think that vibe infects the tone of the show." ■

TRICIA HELFER

"You can't help but look back with a little bit of feeling how lucky you were. Just to have been able to work with the people that I worked with — great actors and great people, and the directors and the cast and crew — was really just a fantastic experience. It opened up a lot of possibilities for me. It was basically my first show; I'd only been acting for a year. So I just feel incredibly lucky to have been a part of it."

[HOT CYLON ON CYLON ACTION!]

"What if the 1978-style Centurions fought the new ones — who would win?" — Jesse Tovey

There are many iconic images that have come out of *Battlestar Galactica* over the years — the Mk II Vipers, Six's red dress, even the antiquated apparatus in CIC — but surely nothing will stay in the minds of viewers quite as permanently as the sinister vision of robot evolution that is the Cylon Centurions. Huge, menacing and merciless, the new incarnation of these metal monsters trooped into our consciousnesses in the Miniseries — but surely reached their finest (and most terrifying) hour during the final episode 'Daybreak'. In fact, what Gary Hutzel and his team came up with for the finale was so extreme that the visual effects supervisor had a very special description for it…"I coined the phrase 'Hot Cylon on Cylon action' and Michael Rymer loved that," laughs Hutzel.

To get that action right, the team hired a new member, Jesse Tovey, who was specifically tasked with character animation for the finale. Tovey's involvement with *Battlestar Galactica* actually went way back to even before the Miniseries had got off the ground. "I feel like I'm a bookend to the entire *Battlestar Galactica* series," the animator laughs. "Lee Stringer, who initially worked at Zoic Studio for the Miniseries, kind of owed me a favour. We [both] used to work at Foundation Imaging, [and] we tried to get *Battlestar Galactica* while we were still working at Foundation. To do that, I built a Centurion that I designed myself and put on a motion capture stage. We got someone to do some tumbles and I animated that. It looked great, but we didn't get the show. So when he had the opportunity to go to Zoic, Lee was in a position to give me the chance to build the actual Centurion for the Miniseries. It was awesome, but I never got to animate it! In all those years, I never got to animate it until I got onto the crew, finally, for the *Battlestar* finale."

In fact, Tovey almost passed up the opportunity, having been initially told that the position would be for just six to eight weeks. "Doug Drexler, [*Battletar Galactica's* CG supervisor] persuaded me," Tovey explains. "He said, 'This is not what you're used to. Why don't you come down and see what we're doing here, because it really is unprecedented in terms of the creativity that you're going to be asked to bring to this crew. We don't want you to just fill a chair.' If it wasn't for that email from Doug, I never would have been able to animate that Centurion that I built in a professional sitting. I finally got to animate my baby," Tovey laughs. "I finally got to play with it myself!"

In fact, Tovey got to play with far more than just his own model of the Centurion, which had evolved throughout the seasons that *Battlestar Galactica* had been on the air. He also got to mix in some of the classic series-style robots — all

Opposite: Who wouldn't want to be a Cylon if you could look like this?

in all, it really *was* a case of "Hot Cylon on Cylon action", and a level of creative freedom that Tovey had never before experienced on television. "I had never worked in a place that had allowed so much of a contribution to what the action would be," he says. "The writers are very unspecific about certain things because they trust the visual effects crew to come up with something to fill that void. They just give us a very basic description — 'The Colonials are engaged by the Cylons in the Hallway. One of them gets shot' and that's it. They let us just run with it. Everything else about the performance and the little idiosyncrasies of the shot they typically leave to us."

For the finale, everyone naturally wanted something very special — as evidenced by the amount of Centurion effects shots that Tovey was asked to orchestrate. "They had never had such a large slate of character animation shots — there were literally thirty to forty or more shots that had Centurions in them, and typically a show would have thirty to forty [effects] shots total. So it was going to be a huge undertaking."

Though Tovey had just joined the team, the rest of Hutzel and Drexler's people had been thinking long and hard about just how the Centurions would move, think and act in certain situations. And, with three different types of Centurion interacting for the finale, that level of detail was vital information for Tovey to have. "They actually gave me combat home signals and little bits and pieces of reference for combat and all these other things that they wanted to integrate into the show," he recalls. "And everybody else in the office, they had come up with all these little vignettes about combat and types of attacks, and how one Centurion would die versus another. They just sort of unleashed a barrage of information when I first started," Tovey laughs. "We culled together all of this stuff and came up with a behaviour pattern for these various types of Centurions that would interact in different ways."

For example, the team decided that the Red Stripe rebel Centurions who had had their inhibitors removed had now been observing human behaviour for some time and should therefore act a little more human than their enemy counterparts. By contrast, "The older Centurions act very robotic, they don't have that sort of cunning intelligent aspect to them," Tovey explains.

Because the script directions for the CG portions of the action were so vague, Tovey felt free to experiment and introduce some new — and distinctly exotic — actions into the Cylon/Cylon battles. "It's almost mixed martial arts combat," he says, "and that was a big deal for me to throw in there. There was no writing for it; nobody had said anything about it. But it was an interesting way to make them fight. I referenced a lot of *Ultimate Fighting Champion* fights — it sort of imitates that kind of combat. There're actually a few Jujitsu moves that you see in one of two of the shots," he laughs, "and an Aikido grapple technique that's used in the background."

Most of Tovey's innovations met with approval from the producers. In fact, there was just one instance where Ron Moore asked for a specific change. In the scene where the Centurions escort Cavil through the corridors of *Galactica*, Tovey had originally animated original-series style Cylons. "The only major change that Ron Moore made was to make that the newer version of the Centurion, which was fairly straightforward except for the fact that that new Centurion is literally almost two feet taller than the older Centurion. So I could reuse all the motions from those scenes that I had already finished, but all the footsteps were too small. So when they were walking down the hallway, they had this very feminine walk," Tovey laughs. "That took a lot of work to jig around. But the rationale ended up being that the new Centurions were taller and larger, but only in the shoulders. And Cavil was much shorter, so you could see him through the profile. It was a decent call, because you see the character a little better. But it was a lot of work for me!"

The whole show was a lot of work for Tovey, though he describes it as an intensely enjoyable task. One of the biggest challenges was a scene in which Cylons and humans are seen across the corridor from each other during a huge fight — all the CGI elements for which needed to be animated by Tovey, by hand. "There was one shot where you panned away from humans coming down the hallway to a wide open section of the Colony where I think there was a dozen of them fighting — Red Stripes fighting season one Centurions (which is the model that I originally built for the Miniseries) and the old style Centurions that look like the ones from the 1978 series. They're all in one hallway and they're all fighting one another. All of it is this master shot to get one Centurion to lower his machine gun right in the face of a human on the other side of the shot, because we pan back from that Centurion to that human getting shot. It's one of the only times we get that close between humans and Centurions, and it really was a massive undertaking because the plate shot for that was so dark and had a really prominent whip-pan in it. As soon as the camera pans away from humans, it goes to an entirely CG environment. And as soon as they all finish fighting, it pans immediately back to those humans. That shot engaged at least five people for close to a month. I had been animating it for at least a week and a half to two weeks straight, then it went to various other people. There are at least a dozen Centurions completely animated by hand — there's no motion capture at all, all of them fighting in this one hallway."

Another shot that followed this sequence constituted one of the most violent of the series. Network guidelines don't allow a lot of graphic human bloodshed, but those rules don't apply to robots — meaning that Tovey could do what he liked in the Cylon/Cylon battles. "They told me to get really over the top violent with it," he laughs. "So I settled an argument of sorts: there's a fun fanboy question out there: What if the 1978-style Centurions fought the new ones — who would win? And I wanted to answer it! So I basically have the 1978-style Centurions losing in this shot where the Red Stripes are dominating. You can actually see the tide turning with this one shot, because the Red Stripe Centurions overpower the other ones very briefly.

One of them gets his helmet shot off, his head gets blown open — another is just getting punch drunk. And then there's a season one Centurion that's forced to shoot himself in the face. He's trying to shoot his attacker, but his arm gets forced into his own face and he blows his own head off!"

Once again, this entire shot was done by Tovey, by hand. The reason that *Battlestar Galactica* stopped using motion-capture, the animator explains, is that doing character animation by hand is ultimately a lot easier for the visual effects department to control. If, for example, they shot a master on green screen with a motion-control actor and director, and then later decided that it wasn't right and needed changing, they'd have to arrange a date and time that they could reconstruct the green screen, re-hire the director and actor, and choreograph what they wanted all over again. With character animation, however, Tovey could go straight in and start reworking any shot that needed changing. "It was a huge undertaking for me," Tovey admits, "but it was sort of a pre-emptive hiring move for them. I was told that *Caprica* was going to involve a really enormous commitment to character animation because there's a central character who is a robot. So they basically wanted to hire a guy on the finale to see if this guy can handle this kind of workload."

The workload became more complicated when Tovey was asked to break off from working on 'Daybreak' to animate on the *Caprica* pilot, a request he admits he was thrown by. "I was just like, 'What? Are you kidding me?'" he laughs. "*Caprica* was very complicated, but it was just one robot, really, the 'U87'. The others were basically like bowling pins, they were very easy to animate. They wanted to get it done ready for the DVD before it aired, but the finale aired before *Caprica*. It was a funny leap frog schedule that was just brutal."

One of the problems that Tovey faced as a result of cutting from *Battlestar Galactica* to *Caprica* and back again was the very different style of animation required for each show. "The robot from *Caprica*, the U87, is the embodiment of a teenage girl, and there's a very prominent and extremely long shot where she wakes up and she's intellectualising the fact that 'I am no longer in a human body' and that's *acting*. That's a human performance, a very soft, very subtle kind of acting, because you don't have a human face to express the angst of this girl. And that's a very different kind of animation than completely violent rock 'em, sock 'em, knock 'em down violence, and all this manly stuff," he laughs. "It was pretty hard trying to get those gears going again. It had to be done — but it was *a lot* to ask!"

Still, the final result of Tovey's efforts on both shows are an amazing example of computer animation at it's best — and Tovey admits that seeing 'Daybreak' was pretty powerful, particularly since he watched the premiere with the cast and crew, on a cinema-sized screen at a SCI FI channel screening. "I was sitting there laughing because I'm used to seeing my work on a television screen, but we went to the screening and it's a full-size screen," Tovey says. "Seeing this on this full screen just amplified the whole thing!" ■

Opposite: Baltar and his Cylon "messenger".

[WILLIAM ADAMA]

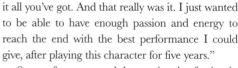

"We've got to roll the hard six. We all go together and as fast as we can."

For William Adama, the final year of his wanderings through space brought despair, heartache and betrayal as well as love and, at last, a kind of peace. Yet despite all that turmoil, the great statesman of the fleet did finally bring the human race to its end — an end far happier than many, including Edward James Olmos, supposed it would be. In fact, Olmos found himself in a similarly momentous position, albeit without the fate of the human race resting on his shoulders.

The actor had taken a risk when he originally signed up for the role of Adama. As he himself says, "Many of my peers don't like to do television. They feel it's beneath them." During the five years of filming in Vancouver, he had become a figurehead for the show's cast. And now, his long journey as the Admiral was coming to an end. "A great marathon runner [wants] to make sure that the last mile is the most proficient in the whole twenty-six mile race," says Olmos. "You start off fast but pace yourself, and in the end you give

it all you've got. And that really was it. I just wanted to be able to have enough passion and energy to reach the end with the best performance I could give, after playing this character for five years."

Season four saw a subtle emotional softening in Adama, as the events — and the relationships — of the past five years affected him. Who would have thought, at the beginning of the series, that the deep-seated conflict between Adama and Roslin would result in such a touching love story? Not Olmos, for sure, although he was very satisfied with the direction that the writers decided to pursue. "It was a love that was well earned," Olmos points out. "The characters earned the relationship, as well as the audience. I think the audience was as happy for us as we were for ourselves — and we were very happy as characters to finally come to terms with our feelings toward each other."

This new emotional side of Adama did not extend to a softening of his stance towards the political life of the fleet. In fact, season four strayed into some disturbing areas of grey as Adama exerts his military power to push through some distinctly un-democratic motions amongst the fleet. "I think all the actions were justified. Whether they were the *right*

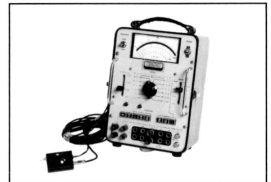

Top: Laura Roslin's costumes: From left to right: Miniseries business suits #1-3, Laura's navy suit.

Above left: Laura's book of Pythian Prophecy and the lighter she uses to burn it, during season four's 'Sometimes a Great Notion'.

Above right: Laura's wireless transmitter, used to send a message to the fleet during Gaeta and Zarek's mutiny.

Left: Elosha's scroll, with intricate carvings, metal and wood accents, and the symbols of the Twelve Colonies.

Above: Adama's dossier from Colonial One, back-up version.

Below: The Medal of Distinction Award presented to Admiral William Adama on his 45th year of service in the fleet, in season three's 'Hero'.

Above: Adama's hero photograph of Zak, Kara and Lee.

Below: Adama's family album, containing photographs of his wife Carolanne and sons Lee and Zak.

Above: Apollo's costumes: From left to right: Gray Digital Camouflage uniform, *Pegasus* Dress Grays uniform, Large Commander uniform from *Pegasus*, bloody costume from season two's 'Scattered'.

Below: Aged version of Lee Adama and Anastasia Dualla photo in Joe's Bar.

Right: Kara Thrace's boxing gear.

Below: Joseph Clark's duffel bag from the season two episode 'Scar'.

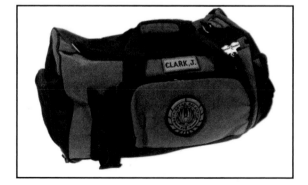

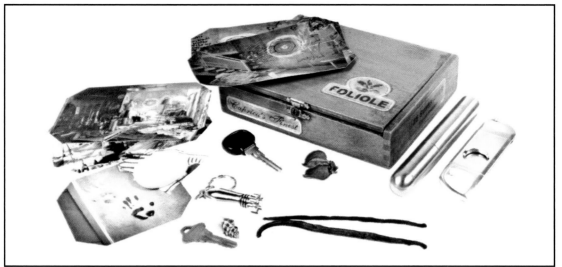

Above: Kara's cigar box with trinkets - hero version. Contents include: two paper photos of Kara's apartment on Caprica, brass house key, stainless steel cigar holder, car key, flat river bed stone, two vanilla beans, small sea shell, piece of torn paper, rocket key chain, seed pod, stainless steel cigar cutter and three real photos of Kara's apartment.

Above & below: Kara's painting on canvas - acrylic with spatula marks.

Above: Kara's painting on canvas - acrylic with spatula marks.
Below: Kara's Hummer Caprica license plates.

Above, from left to right: Head Six's green satin dress (Gucci), Head Six's red suit (custom made), Caprica's Six's sheer black Miniseries outfit.

Left: War Room model: Blackbird.

Below Left: Pyramid - The Boardgame, based on the iconic Pyramid ball game, as seen in Joe's Bar.

Below right: War Room model: Raptor.

way to go or not, that's another issue," laughs the actor. "But I think that everything we did was justifiable, whether it be through what we know as democracy or not. It was a matter of survival. And we made it. It was something that I would not have predicted from the conception of the piece," he adds. "I did not think we would survive."

Olmos' passion for both his character and *Battlestar Galactica* as a whole is obvious. In fact, he says that he still dreams about Adama, and has developed what happened to the character once settled on Earth. "In my own mind, I felt that he ended up building the cabin. He went on living there until Tigh found him and asked for help, and they started an adventure that was unbelievable. I'll talk to people about that some day," he laughs. "It'd be great [to skip forward five years and find out what's going on with them all]. It'd be a great experience, and that's really what I tried to focus in on in that story. It's become a very sad situation now that we're not working with each other any more. It inhabits your dreams. I can't even begin to tell you how gorgeous the experience was. [*Battlestar Galactica*] is one of the greatest experiences of filming I've ever had the privilege of being a part of. It truly was the best experience of my life on television." ∎

[LAURA ROSLIN]

"To those in the fleet and in *Galactica* who would reject this alliance, I am asking you. No, I am begging you to reconsider and place your trust back in those who have brought you this far..."

I t's unusual for an actor to know the final fate of their character before they have even taken the role — but for Mary McDonnell, the one constant in her playing of Roslin has been the knowledge that Laura is dying of cancer. And so the actress went into season four knowing that it would necessarily be the most physically demanding she had yet had to play.

"As an actress, the last season was both exhilarating and so hard that it was truly nice to lift out of it when it was done," admits McDonnell. "When I'm out and about now, people keep saying to me, 'Oh my god, you look so good,' and I go, 'Well, I'm not *dying*, you know!'" she laughs. "I've been dying for four seasons! And it's interesting, because something lifted. You have to play this really interesting game with your psyche. On the one hand you've got to truthfully understand how it feels to have your energy slowly draining and to be working through pain — taking action through pain, thinking through pain. On the other hand you *have* to make sure your brain gets that you're not really sick, because you can create feelings of illness, but you don't want to create the illness, or start messing around with yourself. And so it was just tricky to navigate that."

Roslin's most severe physical downward spiral came immediately following the fleet's discovery of the "true" Earth. Having held up the prospect of this promised planet as a beacon not only for herself but also for the whole fleet, to discover the truth of its devastation was crushing, both mentally and physically. "Ron told me, thank god, that this was not going to be where she would be till the end — hopelessly despondent and dying," McDonnell laughs. "But she had to believe that it was all over. And it all became about shame and guilt. That she had made a huge mistake, and gotten people to trust her and had people killed and had people tortured, and babies died and children, because of this bigger idea of survival of a race that she thought she was responsible for. And suddenly it was like, 'My visions were wrong, it's a failure.' And the feelings of shame and grief were overwhelming. What I was thrilled about, and I will be forever grateful to Ron Moore for, is that he allowed her to die peacefully rather than in a horrible struggle, and that he allowed her to feel that she had finished her job as best she could. Because I honestly do believe that the entire time, the *only* reason she thought she was still alive was to get them to Earth. And I do believe that she felt it was some kind of destined thing, and some kind of strange and difficult karma that she was serving. When she got to finish it and see the land and be on *this* Earth..." The actress laughs, "I loved that last

scene when she says to Adama, 'Fine, call it Earth. Whatever you want'!"

Concluding the saga to everyone's satisfaction would have been impossible, but McDonnell reports herself to be more than happy with how *Battlestar Galactica* finally met its end. "I was very happy with the ending. I really loved it because I felt that the main idea was always that we are continuing to create an illusion which states that we are different from other people. And if we continue to create that illusion, we are going to end up on the first Earth," the actress laughs, "because that creates a diseased planet. But in *Battlestar*, when we had finally embraced the collective, and the other, or the enemy — the reward of that was a beautiful, lush and mysterious planet and a new beginning. And I thought that was a fantastic message. Because to me, that's the only way for the planet to evolve — into a collective, cooperative consciousness. That's *our* hope." ∎

[LEE ADAMA]

"**M**y character is really part of the family drama of the show," says Jamie Bamber, of why he was always confident not only that Lee Adama was not the final Cylon, but why he knew Lee would make it right to the show's conclusion. "There are people who are involved in the whole Cylon thing and that's their story, but my story is Shakespearean family drama. To have messed around with those core characters too much — it just wasn't the way Ron was thinking. He needed those characters to be there at the end."

Along the way, though, the writers conspired to use the fourth season to put Lee through the wringer in every way possible. His emotions were tested right from the opening episode, when Kara Thrace quite literally returns from the dead. Bamber puts Lee's willingness to accept Starbuck back without question down to trauma fatigue: the pilot simply couldn't take any more loss.

"It was good, because Lee is a doubter," says Bamber. "He thinks things through. But he's just come through enough loss and enough problems that he just doesn't want to think too much about this one. He just wants to embrace exactly what he sees and what he wants, which is for her not to be dead. So it's denial. He chooses not to challenge himself and to think too much about it. This one, he just gives up on it. He's had enough, and he takes it at face value. It's denial, but they've been through so much, it's like, 'Well, I don't care any more. Let's just take this for what it is.' He's learned that from his brother['s death]. He's thought about that left, right and centre and back again, and it's not been any help. He's been thinking about it and dwelling on it and stewing — so he just embraces it."

Shortly afterwards, Lee leaves *Galactica* to take his place on *Colonial One* as part of the Quorum. Lee's political career had been bubbling under throughout season three, and Bamber was more than happy for it to be taken further in the show's final season. "I was delighted with that, I thought it was great. I think they'd done the pilot thing to death," confesses the actor, "so for me it was very

important to try something else. The great thing about *Battlestar* is you never know what you're going to do next week. You can do different things and go to different areas — we're not stuck in a mould, and for me it was great to move on. That's what the character's about: he's restless, he's young, he's ambitious and he wants to try different things."

Interestingly, Bamber reveals that he felt that the writers perhaps tried to tie up too many loose ends in the build-up to the finale. "I think we covered too much," he says. "The last three or four episodes are a mad dash to tie up as many plot points as possible. The writers did an amazing job of that, but it was very much done for the fans, and I thought it could have been done much better in a book."

Despite his reservations about that pace, Bamber was very happy with how *Battlestar Galactica* finally came to an end. Part of that satisfaction came from the flash-backs. The actor says that although they weren't surprising to him — he and Katee Sackhoff had long since decided upon their backstory, and if anything what was seen on screen was simply more visceral, rather than vastly different — the opportunity to revisit that time period was welcome and refreshing. "It was nice to see it there, because for me the finale is a meditation on character," he says. "It was lovely to get these people before they were complicated, when they had simple lives. They thought their problems *then* were tough!" he laughs. "That's essentially what each of those flashbacks are — innocent people who thought their lives were full of complex things. And then to see what happens to them, which is what no one would have wished or envisaged, I thought was beautiful. It was very zen and meditative." ∎

[KARA THRACE]

> "Take it from someone who died once; it's no fun."

Kara 'Starbuck' Thrace had always been the wildcard, the unpredictable and volatile soldier with a deathwish. It was always possible that she was going to get herself killed before the show reached its natural end — and, sure enough, the end of season three sees the character's demise. But, with typical *Battlestar Galactica* unpredictability, her death did not mean her end.

"We wanted Kara to have literally have died and been brought back to life," states Moore, "and her not even realising it, being confused about why she was here and who she was and what she was. We wanted it to feed into the larger prophesies of her destiny and the role she was going to play in the piece overall. There was something about her being not one of us, and yet identifiably mortal — here is a person literally resurrected from a literal death — that I thought was really interesting. We wanted it to have mysteries and ambiguities around it. We didn't want to clearly define her character and her origin too specifically, because the more vague you kept it, the more interesting it became."

The question of what Starbuck actually was would resurface later in the season. In the meantime, there was plenty else to keep her occupied — the search for Earth and the revelation of her husband Sam Anders as a Cylon, for starters. The Kara/Sam storyline was one of the most touching of the season, with the two characters fractured understanding of themselves serving to further cement their rather tragic relationship. Sackhoff reveals, however, that the writers' initial idea had been that Anders' reveal as a Cylon would drive Starbuck back into the arms of Lee Adama.

"What's interesting is that the writers had a Starbuck and Apollo relationship that was going somewhere," Sackhoff explained to a packed audience at the Bagdad Theatre in her hometown of Portland, Oregon. "And one of my dearest friends in the world, Michael Trucco, was in a very serious accident. It was a really scary time for not only him and his fiancee and family, but for his friends. I realised at that moment how much he meant to me as a person, and that affected every single moment I had with him on camera. And what he and I realised is that the relationship between Kara and Anders was becoming so much more strong and bonded because of how our friendship changed because of what he had gone through. [So] that's why they ended up together. It was a choice that I couldn't help but make as a person, because I love him so dearly. Had that not happened, Kara might have ended up with Apollo, I don't know."

The undefined nature of Kara's existence, no matter what else occurred to the character during the season, continued to be a main talking point. The resolution, too, was controversial — and, in fact, some would say it was actually no resolution at all.

"One of the most controversial aspects of the finale is how we elected to resolve that story," Eick admits. "It was risky. It was Ron's idea, and the first time I heard it I remember thinking, 'Well, that's going to annoy a lot of people because it's not specific enough.' But if we had tried to make it a more specific, that would have seemed bullshitty or contrived. So why not go with an elegant answer as opposed to a contrived answer? If it winds up feeling insufficient to people, at least you've kept your soul — you haven't turned it into something ridiculous. So that was definitely one that required smoothing out, I guess because, if the show had gone on for another season or two, who knows what we might have come up with to explain Kara Thrace's mysterious return? I'm not suggesting that the explanation the audience has is a stopgap or was something pulled out of our hat at the last second, but I still believe it was a fluid idea. So fluid, that if it had been a year later, the resolution might have been entirely different."

For Sackhoff, however, Starbuck's mysterious nature did not stop the character from finding her own personal salvation, despite the misery she had to go through to get there. "We saw someone, in the beginning, who was willing to die for everyone around her because she didn't value her own life. At the end, we have a character who values existence so much that she's willing to die for other people," Sackhoff told Kat Angus in an interview at the Dose.ca website. "That's a huge change. It changes everything Starbuck does. It makes her compassionate and it makes her circumstances more tragic." ■

[GAIUS BALTAR]

"I am not a priest. I've never even been a particularly good man. I am in fact a profoundly selfish man. But that doesn't matter, you see. Something in the universe loves me. Something in the universe loves the entity that is me."

t's hard to see how Gaius Baltar could have gone through a bigger sea change than he did in *Battlestar Galactica*'s final season. If he had been revealed as one of the final five Cylons, it's likely that few viewers would have been surprised. But instead, he turned to God and became the leader of a monotheistic cult, before finally ending his days as what he had most desperately tried to avoid all his life — a lowly farmer.

"Making Baltar into some sort of Messiah, the object of people's faith and the vehicle for their passion and their beliefs — it just seemed like so far from where we began the character. You'd be failing the character if you *didn't* go there, because the character's nature was of such extremes," says executive producer David Eick, of Baltar's apotheosis. "We had talked about him leading a harem of followers for a long time."

"It was a natural progression," agrees Ron Moore. "He had started out as very secular and atheist, but he'd had an angel or some messenger talking to him constantly about God over the course of the first couple of years. He had gone through an amazing transition — from being vice president to president, then exile, and then he had gone to trial and been acquitted. It felt like there would come a point for this man where he would start to wonder if there really *was* a God, and does this God have a message for him? He could believe there was a God and that he really was something special, because looking back on his life and experiences it certainly seemed as if there was a divine influence, that there was something beyond the strictly rational that had influenced Gaius Baltar's life."

It was a turn of events that James Callis confesses he struggled to assimilate. After all, for Baltar to find God went against almost everything he had been playing since the opening of the series. "I had difficulty with this as a performer," Callis admitted to Chris Dahlen in an interview for the AV Club website. "Because this season, I say one thing, and then I say something totally different. It's what I've been saying to the writers and the directors: 'How do I say this?' For example, one moment [he's saying] 'There [are no gods]! It's all rubbish! They can't help you because they don't exist!' And then the next minute, 'There is a God, and He's our salvation, He loves you.' I'm like, 'Which one of these is it?'

"Then the writing staff and the directors come back to me and go, 'But James, that's what all of these horseshit people talk about! One minute they're talking Latin, and then they change their minds! Just look

at some of these people —' And the name that comes up again and again is Jim Jones. [But] Gaius is not Jim Jones.

"To be honest, I don't believe it. I don't believe it as James Callis, and I don't believe that Gaius believes it either. Because he couldn't."

Working with such contradictions proved difficult for the actor, who goes on to say, "I do find all of those things really tough, to be honest. Belief is everything when you're performing something. If you don't have the belief behind it, then that actually puts a shunt on the character."

Despite his worries over the character's integrity, Callis believes that *Battlestar Galactica*, at its heart, always had something important to say about the world we live in now. "I think it's terribly important," says the actor regarding the parallels that can be drawn between real situations and those explored aboard *Galactica*. "Sorry to quote a boring Shakespeare, but we are holding a mirror up to nature. I think they are brilliant and very, very clever, because it's like looking at an argument in a slightly removed situation. And that then calls into question all of your own allegiances." ■

[NUMBER SIX]

> "She's right, Gaius. The end times are approaching. Humanity's final chapters are about to be written. And you — you will be its author."

Tricia Helfer's journey as Cylon model Six is a long and convoluted one — beginning with the opening of the *Battlestar Galactica* Miniseries, in which the actress delivered the first spoken words in this re-imagined universe. It seems fitting, then, that she was, as 'Head Six' and alongside James Callis as 'Head Baltar', the actress to see the series out. That one little coda also managed to answer a question that had been around ever since the first appearance of Head Six. What was she? A chip in Baltar's head? Or a literal messenger from God? That she turned out to be the latter was, for Helfer, a relief. "I knew she had

to be something like that," the actress laughs. "For five years I filmed not knowing what she was, so I knew it was something to do with that. I didn't think she was a chip in his head — I just didn't feel that was right. There's a scene where Baltar asks, 'What are you?' and she says, 'I'm an angel of God, sent here to protect you.' I took that one line to heart and felt that that's who she was. So it was a nice little validation at the end that she was!"

The actress was also pleased at the resolution reached between Caprica Six and Gaius Baltar. Having begun their relationship before the fall of the Twelve Colonies, that they ended up together was a welcome conclusion for Helfer. "I did expect some kind of resolution between these two characters," she admits. "Though I didn't know what it was going to be. I wasn't surprised that they ended up together, because I think it was one of the love stories throughout the entire show. Obviously there's Anders and Kara, and Lee and Kara, and the President and Adama... But this is one from the very beginning, one of the first ones, so I think it was good that it ended up that way — I felt good about it."

With so many different Sixes in play, there

were plenty of loose ends to be dealt with during the final season. Helfer says that, for the most part, she was happy with how those threads were tied up, though there were some Sixes — all of which the actress created individual characters for — that could have been explored further. "There were a couple of new Sixes introduced at the end — Sonja, the blonde-haired one that finally got a seat in the Quorum, and Lyta. Both of those came in for a couple of episodes and you never saw what happened to them. I would have liked to have seen what happened because I was just getting into them. But that's just my own little thing — they weren't that important as characters. Really, at the end of the day, the most important were Caprica Six and Number Six. Those two were the ones that had the follow-through from the Miniseries all the way to the end.

"I felt very positive about the finale," continues Helfer. "I liked that it *was* a finale. It was a finish. But it didn't tie everything up into a neat little box and say everybody lived happily ever after. We did discuss that, how we all reacted to it when we first read the script. I've heard both sides from fans — some people were very happy with it and some people thought it didn't answer enough, or finish off enough. But I don't like it when everything's put in a neat little box with a bow. For me one of the big things was seeing that these people would actually give up their technology, going back, basically, to living off the land. That was a bit of a shock, but I loved it. I was very satisfied with the finale and I think most of us actors were." ∎

[SAUL & ELLEN TIGH]

"Whether you remember that life or not, at least you must understand what we were trying to do. We wanted to end the cycle of war between man and machine." — Ellen Tigh

Relationships aboard *Battlestar Galactica* rarely run smoothly — one of the show's great hallmarks, in fact, is its ability to portray human partnerships with realistic flaws in a way few television series can bear to. But few are as tumultuous as the marriage of Saul and Ellen Tigh — two people utterly in love and yet utterly unable to live together peaceably. Since we first met them both have seemed hopelessly at odds with themselves. And in season four, we finally found out why.

For Michael Hogan, discovering that Saul Tigh was a Cylon was problematic.

Hogan loves research, and research is how he prepares for a role and builds his character. If he is to play a heart surgeon, he will find a real heart surgeon willing to show him how the surgery is actually performed. If he is to play a teacher, he'll spend time with a real teacher to find out how it's done. But finding out your character is something other than human — well, there are really no physical avenues of research one can take. So how do you prepare?

"When they decided to make Saul Tigh a Cylon, I approached it as mental illness," Hogan told musician Bear McCreary on his blog. "That's the way it was developed, I treated it as a mental illness; there's manic-depression, there's schizophrenia. That was my approach to me being told that I am now playing a Cylon — and how it becomes obvious to me."

This "mental illness", this splitting of personality, is clear in Saul right from the opening of season four, when, during his early fears that he will be unable to stop himself turning on Adama, he hallucinates shooting his commanding officer and friend. For all his faults, Saul Tigh had always been one thing: a steadfastly loyal soldier. So to suddenly be confronted with the idea that he may be a traitor is shattering to him. "That is Tigh's worst fear," says Hogan. "If, in fact, I am a Cylon, what am I capable of? If I'm not the oldest person alive, I'm certainly one of the oldest people alive in the human race. I am certainly the most combat-experienced person alive on that ship. Therefore, if it turns out that I am a Cylon, I'm very dangerous."

Hogan describes Saul as being in pain — of suffering a post-traumatic stress that, rather than lessening over the years, is being added to continually. And one of the biggest additions to that pain was the death, at his own hands, of his wife Ellen.

Somehow, the revelation that Ellen Tigh is in fact the fifth Cylon makes perfect sense. Known as a troublemaker from the get-go, everything Ellen had previously done on *Galactica* was a messy shambles. But when she wakes up on that Basestar a switch has quite literally been flicked in her head.

"Ellen was asleep for the first four years, she had no idea she was a Cylon," explains Kate Vernon of her return as Ellen. "She hadn't downloaded, she hadn't woken up. So when she wakes up, she's fully realised and has complete and total knowledge of the past and the present, and she knows what she wants and how to get it. They wanted me to come in, not with aggression, but just with that knowledge of who she is and what we have to do, that confidence. She comes back with all of that and with much more compassion and clarity. She comes back with a sense of purpose, whereas before she had never had that. She was the XO's wife, and he didn't have any ambition, and it drove her mad. So she was just spinning her wheels and getting into trouble, but she gets to come back with ambition and a sense of purpose and leadership."

Vernon only wishes that she could see more of the characters' stories. "It's got a beautiful poetry in it that I am a Cylon, that Saul is a Cylon, and that we are the oldest married couple in the universe," Vernon laughs. "I thought it was a beautiful ending. Personally, I would love to see where everybody is in three years; I'd be really fascinated. I loved all these characters. I look at *Battlestar* as a massive love story: there's the love story with Adama and Tigh and the ship, there's a love story between Adama and Roslin, the love story between Ellen and Saul, the love story between Kara and Anders, the love story with Galen and Sharon and Cally — it deals with such a core level of humanity. Because who are we without relationships? I'm happy at the whole arc of this and the rising of the phoenix of Ellen Tigh!" ∎

[ATHENA / BOOMER]

"Too much confusion."

Who would have expected the troubled partnership of Sharon and Karl Agathon to have such a happy ending? Not Grace Park, that's for sure. "I totally thought one of them was going to die, or they were both going to die," she laughs. "I thought that Hera was going to live, like in a heroic, mythical type of story where someone's born into nobility and separated from their family, and it's much more of a struggle. I thought that something like that would happen to Hera, and she would have to grow up without her parents. So reading the finale, when Sharon leaves [the wounded] Helo, I was like, 'Oh no!' I just knew that

he died, right then; I completely jumped to that conclusion. Then I watched the finale sitting between Tahmoh and his dad, and his dad was like, 'Oh my god, I thought that was the end of you, too!' I don't think a lot of people thought they would have made it to the end, so once again Ron surprised people by doing something that they hadn't expected."

For Boomer, however, a happy ending really was impossible. She had always, Park feels, been searching for her place in the universe. Most of her mistakes had been a part of that search, and in season four the repercussions of those mistakes could no longer be avoided, despite her final gesture in returning Hera to her parents.

"I don't know if bringing the child back is really enough to redeem her for everything else that she's done," says Park. "But certainly that's the best thing she could have done and, knowing what Hera stands for, quite possibly that's the best decision she's ever made. When she brought Hera back she knew what would likely happen. She knew that she was walking right into enemy territory — especially after what she did with Helo just days before! She had made a lot of mistakes and her guilt had caught up with her and she didn't want to live

like that any more. I think she quite willingly gave her life over, feeling that she'd done enough damage and this was probably the best way to go out. I felt it was a willing sacrifice. She was apologising with her life."

Park confesses that, for her, letting go hasn't been as easy. It's fair to say her role on *Battlestar Galactica* had been her most challenging to date, and the immersive nature of the series' five-year shoot was, for a time, all consuming. "It's changed me," she says. "I've grown a lot with *Battlestar*, it's given me many, many experiences. I've experienced parts of the world that I don't think I would have ever seen, or even had awareness of. And it's given me such an appreciation of people and relationships and storytelling — film crews, professionalism, ethics and kindness. I didn't know for the longest time whether I was going to say goodbye, and have closure. It was only a few days ago, when someone on my new show asked, 'Do you miss *Battlestar*?' It was kind of weird, and I had to think for a second. And I said, 'No.' Of course I miss it and love it, but there wasn't that kind of hurt that I've had in my chest for two years, where I could just cry easily about it. While we were still shooting it, in the middle of it, when the strike came, when the ending came, when the finale came — there were so many parts where I thought, 'When am I going to stop being sad about this show? It is over!'" she laughs. "I'm like 'Oh my god, am I ever going to be able to let this go?' So knowing that I did felt great. Because I'll have other good experiences, but it'll always be with me. And if I forget I can always go put on a DVD!" ∎

[KARL 'HELO' AGATHON]

"You want me to let it go? You're the one who can't let it go. The ship is dead!"

For Tahmoh Penikett, the final year of *Battlestar Galactica* marked a milestone in his career. The young actor had, he readily acknowledges, really cut his teeth on the series, which had been the first big acting job of his career, and he felt a great desire to see the show out in the best way possible. "By the time we got to season four, Helo and Athena's family had been through so much. From a personal level as an actor, I just wanted to continue to be challenged, and to see Helo taken to his breaking point — and he really is. He almost snaps near the end, the pressure is just too much. He's such a strong, stoic character, but ultimately everyone has a breaking point."

As discussed elsewhere in this book, Ron Moore revealed that the network had noticed Helo's absence from scripts early on in the season, prompting the writer to add the character into events occurring on the *Demetrius*. As the post-strike filming on the second half of the season rolled around, Penikett had been one of the actors released from his contract to enable him to film a new project in Los Angeles — Joss Whedon's *Dollhouse*. As a result, Penikett acknowledges that Helo doesn't appear as much in the latter half of the final season as he would have liked. "I was very happy with the direction they took my character," says the actor. "They were constantly improving the amount of screen time I had and how relevant Helo was to the storyline and I'm really flattered by that. It was an honour to have more screen time and the opportunity to act with any of our exceptional cast. There were some points in the fourth season where I wished I could have been a little bit more involved with the story-line, but the fact was that I couldn't be because I was being released to shoot another pilot. And that's a testament, too, to our line producers for releasing me, in a very important season, to go and do another show."

Regardless of how much physical screen time

Helo saw, the fact was that the character — and the rest of his family unit — were a vital part of the season's revelations. Some of the show's most powerful scenes were told through the relationship of those characters; for example the scene in which a distraught Helo pleads with Admiral Adama to give him a ship in which to search for his kidnapped daughter. "When I read that scene, I got really emotional right away," he recalls. "I knew exactly where he was at that point — he's falling apart, he's starting to slip, he's almost going to crack. I don't know if anyone realises, but I'm playing that scene quite intoxicated, too. Helo's been hitting the bottle for a couple of days. When it comes to situations like that, you just have to open yourself up to it. And when you are being directed by and are acting with one of the greatest actors out there, Edward James Olmos, who directed that scene and that episode, you're even more confident going into it. It's awesome to dance with the best!"

Penikett was also fascinated by the parallels that Helo's own personal troubles drew with the situation of the fleet at that moment — which was, for him, an indication of just how great the writing behind *Battlestar Galactica* was. "I just find it so interesting that everyone's experiencing the same thing but in different ways," says Penikiett. "Everyone's falling apart, we've been taken to our threshold. Humanity's just been tested too much and is losing all hope and faith. I think that's one of the things that I realised when I first read that scene."

Helo almost didn't survive, though — and when he first read the script for 'Daybreak', Penikett actually thought that his character had failed to make it to the end. Having discussed with Michael Rymer the idea that Helo could be one of the unlucky few not to make it to 'Earth', and, after explaining why he thought Helo should survive, Penikett had no idea whether or not the producers had listened to his pleas. "I gave my two bits, and then Michael said, 'Okay, well, I'll talk about it with Ron and David and we'll get back to you.' And then when I read that last script, they actually had me! When I read about Helo getting shot in the leg and you see him bleeding out... and then it was just left... I was like, 'Oh my god — did I just die?!'"

Thankfully, that turned out not to be the case — although that scene did constitute the last full scene Penikett shot for the series. "Even talking about it makes me emotional," he laughs. "It was an incredibly sad, proud and joyous moment. [*Battlestar* is] such an important part of my life, and I'm just really impressed at the way that Ron wrote that last episode, the last three hours. I think it's epic. It's beautiful." ■

[SAMUEL T. ANDERS]

"See you on the other side."

"I t was a bit overwhelming at the beginning, because it just didn't make sense," confesses Michael Trucco, of discovering that he would be playing Anders as a newly self-aware Cylon for *Battlestar Galactica*'s final year. "On two different planes, I didn't know what to do, because a season and a half prior to that, we had established that Anders had been a staunch advocate for the Resistance — he was one of the loyalists. And then this curveball was thrown at us. I think that was probably by design. The point of good television drama is to throw as many curveballs as you can at your audience. But when the *actors* don't see it coming," he laughs, "it's pretty surprising. It's like, 'What? Me? Why?!' So it was a lot to swallow in the beginning. I just decided that the quest for identity and uncertainty really played well into Anders' development. There was this constant unease, a quest for identity and this longing to place himself somewhere."

Season four — particularly the second half — was massively challenging for Trucco. As discussed in the introduction to this book, during the extended hiatus of the writers' strike he had been involved in a car accident in which he broke his neck. Doctors still don't know how he managed to avoid paralysis. It really is a miracle that he regained mobility so completely, not to mention that he returned to work on *Battlestar Galactica* so relatively soon after the accident. But, of course, not long after filming rolled back into production, Trucco discovered that Anders was to suffer a life-threatening injury himself.

"I was nervous about coming back at first," he admits, "not because of the injury so much but because I was worried that I would just be a wallflower because everybody would be so apprehensive about using me. That was a crazy time. The sequence [in which Anders was shot] was fun in the sense that it was good to be back on set and back at work, and I loved the way it went down. But it got really difficult at times, emotionally, in the hospital bed sequences before he goes into the permanent coma. Just being hooked up to all that equipment — even though they're all props — being in a hospital bed so soon after the accident stirred up a lot of emotion, because it was just a little too close to home. Being there with wires hooked up to your wrists and hands and arms, and machines beeping and stuff taped to your chest... It was kind of reminiscent of what I had gone through three months earlier. So there were some days where I had to take some deep breaths and calm myself down. But that's what you do: you tap into something and the reaction is usually good."

One of *Battlestar Galactica*'s many strengths is how it often distils humanity's larger issues into microcosms played out within the lead characters' relationships. This is particularly true of the connection between Sam and Kara, whose volatile relationship

reaches a crescendo as things fall apart within the fleet. "That volatility was the hinge of the relationship," says Trucco. "I can't put words in Katee's mouth, but Kara Thrace had a pattern of driving people away from her. That was kind of the characterisation of Starbuck, to keep people at arm's length. For me, playing Anders, I refused to accept that. And even though we had ups and downs and there were times when he just walked away, ultimately, he always came back to her, and it felt like she always came back to him. And that closure at the very end, the scene where they have their last goodbye — I felt that you could see the walls of both characters break down. He steps out of his daze for a second and he says: 'I'll see you on the other side.' There was a moment of recognition, and it was a really beautiful moment on screen for us. It was really quite harmonious, and that, to me, encapsulated their relationship perfectly. Ultimately, through all that bullshit, there was closure and togetherness." ∎

[SUPPORTING CHARACTERS]

"You swore the same allegiance! What happened to your oath? For seven years I have done my frakking job and for what? To take orders from a Cylon? To let machines network our ship? No, you... you are not the leader you were when we started. You're just a sad old man who has let his heart and his affection for a Cylon cloud his judgment."
— Felix Gaeta

As far as *Battlestar Galactica* is concerned, it's difficult to work out which characters should be considered as 'supporting'. There is no such thing as a less important character in this show, and each, particularly in the final season, proved themselves to be integral to events.

Take **Felix Gaeta**, for example, whose arc in season four was possibly the most unpredictable, yet ultimately vital. The character had been part of the *Battlestar Galactica* landscape since the Miniseries and was an intensely loyal member of Adama's crew. Yet season four saw him attempt a mutiny, lose a leg, and ferment a rebellion that would eventually be his downfall.

"I did think that maybe he might snap, but I don't think I ever predicted that it would be as extreme as it was," recalls Alessandro Juliani, of what he envisioned for Gaeta in season four. "He'd been stewing for a long time, to be sure, and he had no shortage of motivation. A person can only take so much. But I never expected that he would upset the applecart so completely and overthrow Adama. I think that's one of the greatest [shocks] of all. This figure that he idolised completely at the beginning of the Miniseries, who was a father figure to everyone in that crew, to turn on him was the ultimate act of betrayal."

Despite the shocking nature of Gaeta's revolt and death, Juliani feels that it was absolutely the right direction in which to take the character. "It totally made sense to me," he says. "Of course, there's the initial shock, but I understood, in the grand arc of the show, how it was necessary for that to happen. I was definitely a little sad to not be there at the end, both personally and for Felix, to not get to have some reward, some pay-off. Even though I think Felix does find a certain level of peace before he's executed, it would have been nice for him and Hoshi to build a cabin together, too! And for me, I had mixed feelings. I think if there had to be a demise for him, I couldn't have written a better one. But at the same time, watching the finale, there was without a doubt a feeling of missing out on something and not being a part of the climax of the story. I missed it, and Felix missed it. But overall, just having had the gift of those people and that show is more than enough."

Chief Tyrol was another character that had been part of the *Battlestar Galactica* universe since the Miniseries. The conclusion of season three had revealed him as one of the final five Cylons — a revelation that at first did not best please Aaron Douglas. "I initially really disliked the idea, as I felt that they were taking a character that the fans really related to and had quite an affection for and were making him into something they would shun and dislike," Douglas told Bear McCreary, in an interview on the composer's blog. "I also realised that no one would humanise the Cylons more than the Chief so I appreciated the choice from that standpoint."

As season four progressed, Douglas confesses that he warmed to the idea — mainly as a result of the extraordinary arc that the Chief travelled during the season. From Cally's shocking death and the discovery that Nicky was not his son to Boomer's return and his response to Tory's treachery, there were few stones not hurled at the Chief during the show's final year.

Ron Moore has since revealed that there were storylines they had intended to explore for the character but had to abandon because of time constraints. For example, in the aftermath of Cally's death, the writers had originally planned to have the Chief investigate, becoming obsessed with the impossible circumstances of her 'suicide'. Despite the fact that this thread was dropped, Douglas was pleased that there was at least some resolution in the finale, namely Tyrol's reaction when he discovered Tory's culpability in Cally's death. "The Chief gets his revenge," he

told interviewers at the Dallas All-Con. "He has a mini-postal moment. It's very exciting, it was very fulfilling. It was good for me."

Overall, and despite his initial chagrin at the unexpected path his character took, Douglas declares himself to be happy with the Chief's lot. And for himself is simply happy to have been a part of a show that he feels made television history.

"The end of *Battlestar Galactica* for me," the actor told McCreary, "is more than just the ending of a television program that will not only stand the test of time but I feel will be looked back upon as a show that fundamentally changed the genre itself. It truly is lightning in a bottle. But it is also a profound chapter in the book of my life."

Another character whose life had been turned upside down at the conclusion of season three was that of **Tory Foster**. A relatively new character (brought in as a result of Billy Keikeya's exit as the President's aide), Tory had, up until the revelation of her Cylon nature, been somewhat in the background. Season four gave her a starring role — one that required her to cosy up to Gaius Baltar. For actress Rekha Sharma, Tory's seduction of the doctor was far harder to reconcile herself to than the idea that her character was a Cylon. "My first thought was '*No* frakkin' way!'" she recalls, of reading the script that put Tory in bed with Baltar. "Everyone hated Gaius Baltar and Tory was no exception. This made me realise both how desperate and how strong she was, to be able to sleep with the enemy... and, of course, things got more and more twisted as she tries to wrestle with the truth of who and what she is."

Tory's end came with shocking finality, as the Chief snaps her neck in a fit of rage. Sharma didn't completely agree with Tyrol's response to Tory's murder of Cally — to her mind, Tory and the Chief had had a profound connection 2,000 years ago which led her to take such action in the first place. "That was a shocking way to go, for sure," she agrees. "I kept thinking, 'Yes, I betrayed him, but it was desperate times and desperate measures, and if we'd been in love for 2,000 years...' I don't know. At the end of the day, you've just got to go with it. A lot of things in life don't make sense to our limited puny minds! I'm so glad I was part of *Battlestar*. It was a lot of fun, I loved the story, and the lasting friendships are worth their weight in gold." ∎

[THE AUCTION]

> "They have been the best prop and costume auctions of all time, and I'm very proud of that." — Alec Peters

O ver the five years that *Battlestar Galactica* was on air, it accumulated a remarkably large store of props, sets and costumes, most of which had been produced specifically for the show. There were blasters, dogtags, insignia pins, paintings, helmets, books, pads of paper, statues... Name an object, and at some point during the show's history it's likely that one of the craft departments had been called on to make one. So, when the series concluded, the question was, what to do with this vast resource. Having seen the success of Paramount's huge *Star Trek* auction in 2006, Universal realised that something similar could be perfect for *Battlestar Galactica*. And that's where Alec Peters stepped in.

Peters holds one of the largest collections of *Star Trek* props and costumes in the world. As an avid science fiction fan himself, he knew exactly what the *Battlestar Galactica* audience would be looking for from an auction — and, as a successful entrepreneur, he knew how to deliver it. "When *Battlestar* was coming to a close, I contacted Richard Hatch, who's a good friend of mine, and said, 'Hey Richard, find out who's in charge of liquidating everything once the show's over.' He put me in touch with Ron French, the line producer, who put me in touch with Kurt Ford at Universal Studios. They knew they wanted to do an auction as they had seen the success of *Star Trek* and knew they had a lot of good stuff. So I pitched Kirk along with two other companies, and won the contract."

And so Propworx was launched, a company specialising in selling props and costumes in both live and internet auctions. It was decided that there would be two live *Battlestar Galactica* auctions, the first of which would take place at the Pasadena Convention Center in California on the 17 and 18 January 2009.

"We went up to the studio [in Vancouver] for three months, myself and my assistant," Peters recalls. "We had offices at the studio, and our job was cataloguing everything, getting everything ready to produce a catalogue for the auction. It was a pretty big task," he laughs.

Peters and his team were aiming to produce more than a standard auction

Below: War room models: Mark II Vipers.

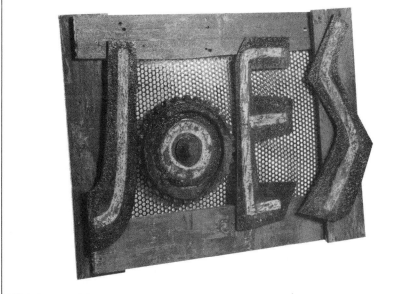

Above: Adama's ship model — the model destroyed by a grief-striken Adama, after Starbuck's death.

Left: The sign for Joe's Bar.

event, and spent a lot of time putting together catalogues that would appeal even to those fans who couldn't splash out and buy an actual piece of memorabilia. Featuring beautifully detailed photographs and information about all the available props, sets and costumes, the catalogues themselves provide a valuable record of *Battlestar Galactica*'s run. "People can still buy the catalogues, which are really works of art unto themselves," he says. "The cast and crew were involved in the first auction in that we really made the first one about how the show was created. So in the first catalogue there are interviews with all the department heads — props, costumes, set decoration, construction, art… It was really important to incorporate them into the auction and make them know that were valuable to the whole event."

Fans were also involved in the event itself, as Peters explains. "We worked with The Colonial Fleet, which is the biggest *Battlestar Galactica* fan club. They came and dressed up in costume and were our ushers and our security. It was just awesome!"

The second auction was held in Pasadena between 8 and 10 May 2009, and attracted just as much attention as Propworx's first event. The size and scale of the auctions, not to mention their success, has come as no surprise to Peters, who knew immediately that the quality of the items available coupled with the massive interest in *Battlestar* would make these events hugely popular. "My vision was to really hold something special," he explains. "Universal really rolled out the red carpet as well — their publicity and marketing teams did a fantastic job."

There were thousands of items that fans were desperate to get their hands on. But from each auction, two items really stood out, and both sold for an amazing price. "The Adama Cylon war painting sold in the first auction for $17,000, and that was obviously very, very popular. That was very iconic," says Peters, speaking of the painting that hung in Adama's office during the show's entire run. "We have since done a limited edition of print of it, and now that's very popular too. The red dress [as worn by Tricia Helfer as Head Six] was the most expensive item we sold — it went for $23,000 dollars in the second auction."

Above right : Head Six's iconic red dress.

Below: Adama's painting of 'The Cylon War' by *Galactica* artist Ken Rabehl.

Propworx also had five of the smaller Colonial ships up for auction, including a Viper, a Raptor and the Blackbird 'Stealth Viper', named for Laura Roslin, all carrying estimates of between $25,000 and $80,000. "Because of the economy and because of the size of them, they haven't sold," Peters reports. "We sold one of the ships, a Viper, to a collector in France. But we're working on the rest, and hopefully they may wind up in the Sci Fi Museum in Seattle, Washington, or maybe the National Aerospace Museum in Houston. We're looking at all our options as to how to preserve those ships."

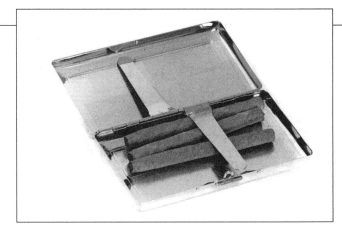

Above: Baltar's cigarette case and hand-rolled cigarettes.

Below: The auction team with the Blackbird 'Stealth Viper', named for Laura Roslin.

Preserving these items is really one of the main reasons that these auctions are so important. In years gone by, props and sets would have simply been broken up, or reused in some fashion for other productions, as studios usually don't have the room to keep such materials indefinitely. By auctioning off these items, *Battlestar Galactica* passes into the care of fans who truly respect and want to preserve the memory of the show. It was this notion that finally persuaded executive producer Ronald D. Moore that the auction was a good idea. "It was very emotional," Moore recalls. "When it was first proposed to me, I thought it was strange to have someone sifting through my attic and selling all my childhood things. But as I thought more about it, I realised that people would cherish them more and take care of them, and they wouldn't just languish in a warehouse. And then I embraced it."

In fact, Moore ended up buying a memento from the series himself — Gaius Baltar's cigarette case. Peters, too, confesses that having been so closely involved with the auctions, he has found his once exclusively *Star Trek* collection expanding to include a few *Battlestar Galactica* items. "I'm a huge *Battlestar Galactica* fan. I was a fan of the original show back in '78, and then I became friends with Richard Hatch, so we would chat about it. The show is just the best science fiction show on TV in history. And I'm a *huge Star Trek* fan — *Star Trek: Deep Space Nine* is my favourite TV show of all time. But *Battlestar Galactica* is the best sci fi show of all time."

With most of the thousands of items available now safely re-housed with loving

Above: Adama's costumes, from left to right: Duty Blues uniform, Dress Grays uniform and Digital Camouflage outfit.

Right: *Galactica* Top Gun beer stein hero version (left) and double (right).

owners, Peters anticipates that Propworx will continue selling the last items through to the middle of July 2009. After that, though the catalogues will still be available, most of the *Battlestar Galactica* materials will have sold out. "I really think that it fulfilled my vision of what I wanted this to be," Peters says simply. "They have been the best prop and costume auctions of all time, and I'm very proud of that." ∎

Battlestarprops.com

[*BATTLESTAR* AT THE UNITED NATIONS]

"There is but one race. So say we all. *So say we all!*"
— Edward James Olmos

As if it wasn't already clear that *Battlestar Galactica* had made an immeasurable impression on viewers the world over, in 2009 the series was given another, perhaps even greater chance to impact on the world at large. On 17 March, producers Ronald D. Moore and David Eick, along with series stars Edward James Olmos and Mary McDonnell were invited join Craig Mokhiber (Deputy Director, New York Office, Office of the High Commissioner for Human Rights) and other UN personnel on a panel at the United Nations building in New York. Co-presented by the UN Public Information Department and the US SCI FI Channel, the event gathered an audience of around 500 attendees, 100 of them New York high school students, as the panel discussed some of the tough issues that had been raised during *Battlestar Galactica*'s run — issues including torture, terrorism, and religious war. The discussion was moderated by actress and UNICEF Ambassador Whoopi Goldberg, a self-confessed fan of the show. "It's such an honour, to be here at the UN," she said in her opening remarks, "[and] to be here with a show that I believe is probably one of the best-written shows on television."

"It was totally surprising," Moore admits, of his first thoughts when the invitation was made for him to join the two-hour discussion and question and answer session. "[But] the Secretary General's office had put out this idea of doing outreach to the creative community, to try to advance the UN's mission, and to get people to think and talk about what the UN is all about. They wanted to touch base with the creative community as a way of helping them with that."

"This was an attempt to be able to use pop culture, to a certain extent, to help articulate their policy," explains Mary McDonnell. "And they so loved the show."

The fact that *Battlestar Galactica* had never shied away from difficult issues such as suicide bombing and genocide made it a perfect crucible in which to try out the UN's notion. And, as Edward James Olmos points out, the fact that these issues were already being discussed by fans the world over made the UN doubly interested. "When the people at the UN got hold of the programme and started to look at it, they started to see the relationship between what we were trying to bring awareness to and what they were trying to bring awareness to," he says. "So they decided to bring more attention to what they do by bringing us into the assembly and by allowing us to comment on the show and what it was doing. And by doing so, they in turn could speak about what they were doing on the same issues."

The panel began with a series of clips from *Battlestar Galactica*, and a brief address by Craig Mokhiber, who drew parallels between the peaks and troughs of the human/Cylon conflict and what is happening in reality today.

"Defining human beings as being 'The Other' so that we can dehumanise them and ultimately destroy them — this is a common theme of our reality, and a common theme of our science fiction as well," he pointed out. "We are all Cylons — every one of us is a Cylon and every one of us is a Colonial and you have to get rid of the idea of good guys and bad guys. Because the truth is, today I may be victimised, tomorrow I may be a victimiser. And the only solution to that is to operate on the basis of a common set of norms that are universally agreed, that apply to me and apply to you — whether you like me or not. Whether you *agree* with me or not."

The panel and the audience alike were of course not unaware that this principle had ultimately been the key to the survival of the human race in *Battlestar Galactica*. Despite all that had occurred between the two sides, the ultimate solution, as seen in the finale, 'Daybreak', was to lay down arms and move forward, regardless of what had happened in the past. This, Mokhiber added, was not currently happening in reality. "In the film clip, when I heard the actress scream, 'We're going the wrong way'," he said, speaking of the scene in which Starbuck, locked in the brig, can feel the path to Earth slipping away from her, "I wanted to join her. We *are* going the wrong way. We need to get back to the essential mission of the Universal Declaration [of Human Rights]… We are all entitled to a social and international order in which all the rights and freedoms in the Universal Declaration of Human Rights can be fully realised, regardless of race, sex, language, religion — or I suppose, your place in the Cylon/Colonial divide. So I would suggest that this is the mythical 'Earth' for which we are all searching, the mythical Earth for which the characters in the series have been searching. And it is very much the vision of the UN as well, only for us it is not a myth, it is absolutely essential and our reason for being here."

In a stirring beginning to the further discussion, Olmos immediately took issue with Mokhiber's choice of words — though not, ultimately, his intent. "I still find it incredible that we still use the word race as a cultural determinant…" the actor began. "I detest what we have done to ourselves. Out of a need to make ourselves different from one other, we have made the word 'race' a way of expressing culture. There's no such thing… as a Latino race, an Asian race, an indigenous race, a Caucasian race. There is no such thing. There's only one race, and that's what the show brought out. That is the human race, period." The reason the word 'race' has come to mean 'culture', Olmos went on to state, was that it made it easier for one group of humans to kill another. "There is but one race," he concluded, before shouting, "So say we all. *So say we all!*"

The audience responded in kind, shouting the actor's words back to him in a show of emotion and passion likely rarely seen in that conference hall. "It was incredible," Olmos says. "I was very grateful to be a part of that."

"It was a remarkable experience," agrees McDonnell, of the event as a whole. "I think the UN and the SCI FI Channel publicity department, in conjunction with Ron, did a

really wonderful job of looking at *Battlestar* and culling scenes that were appropriate to specific areas of the United Nation's mission. The people that came from the UN to speak were phenomenally eloquent, and really quite inspiring and outstanding. Whoopi Goldberg, who is a huge fan of the show, did a fantastic job moderating, the questions were right on… As an actor you feel very, very humbled by an event like this. Something that you love to do, that you work very hard at but is nevertheless entertainment suddenly brings you to a place where you're able to be a part of and be educated by and stimulated by some of our really great thinkers. People who are truly devoted to the planet, to the human race. And their day jobs are real! I just felt very fortunate to be able to be included in something like that."

Fans interested in watching the entire panel will be pleased to know that a full video of the event is available on YouTube. ∎

[ACKNOWLEDGEMENTS]

There is an extraordinary wealth of fantastic *Battlestar Galactica* material on the web, and this book would have been impossible to put together without it…

First of all, *Battlestar Galactica* composer Bear McCreary's blog, which can be found at **www.bearmccreary.com/blog/**. Bear very kindly allowed me to use cuts from his site, which is a vital treasure trove of material, not to mention a fascinating view from inside the industry. Definitely recommended for anyone from casual fans to film students and professionals (whether or not you're specifically interested in music), I guarantee you'll learn at least one thing you didn't know in every one of Bear's episode-by-episode blogs.

Maureen Ryan's wonderful blog *The Watcher* for the *Chicago Tribune* is a must for any fan, featuring fantastic reviews, debates, and interviews with the writers and producers. She writes about far more than just *Battlestar*, but you can find her show-specific material at:
http://featuresblogs.chicagotribune.com/entertainment_tv/battlestar_galactica/
Maureen was also very gracious in letting me use cuts from her work. Thanks a million, Maureen!

Where better to learn about a show than from the creator's mouth? Ron Moore's podcasts are a font of knowledge and entertainment — download them from:
http://www.scifi.com/battlestar/downloads/podcast.php

Throughout the show's run, the excellent ComicMix website featured regular chats with writer Mark Verheiden, which I found very useful. Visit them at:
www.comicmix.com

As a jumping-off point for research, it's impossible to do better than the *Battlestar Wiki*, which has an exhaustive amount of detailed information about the entire franchise, old and new. Fill your boots at: **www.battlestarwiki.org**

Thanks must also go to Alec Peters at Propworx, the official auction house for *Battlestar Galactica* merchandise. What I wouldn't give for Starbuck's flight suit… or one of the Raptors, for that matter. I suspect its interior would be bigger than my writer's garret. We mere mortals might not be able to own a piece of *Galactica* memorabilia, but we can still swoon over the fabulously detailed catalogues — visit **www.propworx.com** for your copy.

— Sharon Gosling